Gila River Indian Community
Anthropological Research Papers
Number 1

Pollen and Micro-Invertebrates from Modern Earthen Canals and Other Fluvial Environments along the Middle Gila River, Central Arizona

Implications for Archaeological Interpretation

Karen R. Adams, Susan J. Smith, and Manuel R. Palacios-Fest

Gila River Indian Community
Cultural Resource Management Program
Sacaton, Arizona

About the Authors

KAREN R. ADAMS, PhD, is a Southwestern U.S. archaeobotanist and consultant for the Gila River Indian Community, Cultural Resource Management Program, Sacaton, AZ 85247

SUSAN J. SMITH is a senior archaeological palynologist at the Laboratory of Paleoecology, Bilby Research Center, Northern Arizona University, Flagstaff, AZ 86011.

MANUEL R. PALACIOS-FEST, PhD, specializes in micro-invertebrate analyses, and is senior researcher and owner of Terra Nostra Earth Sciences Research, 3220 West Ina Road #8105, Tucson, AZ 85741.

Cover: Snaketown Historical Canal, courtesy of Arizona State Museum, University of Arizona, H. Teiwes, photographer

Printed in the United States of America

ISBN : 978-0-9723347-0-9

TABLE OF CONTENTS

List of Figures

List of Tables

FOREWORD

This volume represents the first, of what we plan to be a long lasting and significant series of research papers, dedicated to the study and elucidation of the prehistoric and historic peoples who inhabited the middle Gila River valley. It seems only fitting for Gila River's inaugural anthropological research paper to present environmental studies of modern-earthen irrigation canals initially constructed in the 1930s and to consider their applicability for understanding prehistoric Hohokam and historical Akimel O'odham canal systems occupying the same landscape. The present-day Pima Indians, Akimel O'odham, and their ancestors, the Hohokam, have been long known as the master farmers of the Sonoran Desert who constructed and maintained for a thousand years or more extensive irrigation canal systems within the Gila and Salt River valleys.

Over the next quarter century, the Gila River Indian Community will complete the construction of the Pima-Maricopa Irrigation Project, which will provide water to a minimum of 146,000 acres of farmland. Delivering water to such a large project area will require the construction of over 80 miles of main stem canal and ultimately 2,400 miles of secondary and lateral canals. The construction of this extensive irrigation system and resulting on-farm development will impact important large prehistoric and historic settlements and associated irrigation systems. However, it will provide the Gila River Cultural Resource Management Program with a unique opportunity to utilize the work by Adams, Smith and Palacios-Fest to better document and understand the evolution and use of irrigation systems within the middle Gila River valley.

John C. Ravesloot, Coordinator
Cultural Resource Management Program

x

ACKNOWLEDGMENTS

We would like to thank the Gila River Indian Community for allowing this study on their lands. The GRIC Cultural Resources Management Program, coordinated by John C. Ravesloot, recognizes the value of modern analog studies and encouraged and supported this research.

Able field assistance to acquire the canal samples and other fluvial samples was provided by archaeologists M. Kyle Woodson, Mark Brodbeck, and Tim Watkins. M. Kyle Woodson served as liaison with hydrological engineers and provided information contained in Tables 5 and 6, as well as other general advice. Randy Shaw, irrigation engineer, provided modern terminology for describing canal ranks. Archaeologists Andrew Darling, Glen Rice, and John Ravesloot all provided critical reviews of an earlier draft, as did external reviewers Patricia Crown, Suzanne K. Fish, Keith Kintigh, Teresita Majewski, and John D. Speth.

The desert lands of the Gila River Indian Community have been farmed through time by groups that developed a range of successful water management strategies suited to an extremely arid landscape (Figure 1). To ensure that water reached crops in fields, the grandest and most labor intensive of all the approaches has been the construction of extensive irrigation canal systems. These canal systems have carried spring snow melt and summer rain water from the impermanent Gila and Salt Rivers for miles across the wide, fertile valleys of Central Arizona. The evidence of many prehistoric canals is still preserved in the region, and often the focus of archaeological excavation (Figure 2a; Woodson 2002). These ancient canals, with their succeeding layers of fill (Figure 2b; Woodson and Neily 1998), provide a unique opportunity to reconstruct both aspects of the environment, as well as some of the strategies of irrigation agriculturalists in the past.

Figure 1. Rivers play a critical role in bringing water to the very arid Sonoran Desert Landscape

The following examination of pollen, molluscs, ostracodes, and sediment particle size from modern Gila River earthen canals and other fluvial locations on Gila River Indian Community (GRIC) lands is intended to provide analog data for interpreting prehistoric and

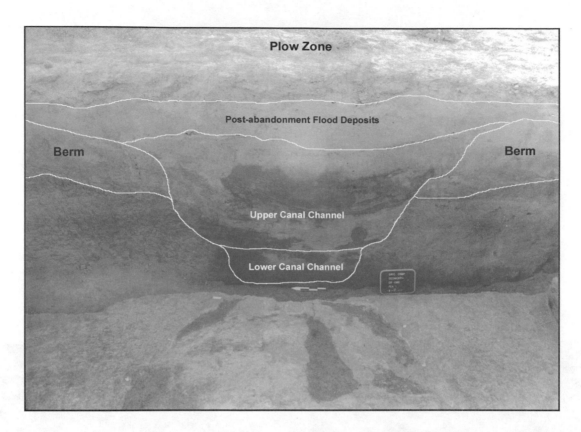

Figure 2. (a) Large, ancient irrigation canal, visible in profile (Woodson 2002). (b) Another ancient canal, excavated by seven individual fill layers, site GR-556. Scale bar and north arrow marked in 10-cm increments (Woodson and Neily 1998).

Figure 3. Cleaning co-op ditch, 1917

historical canals. The Hohokam living along the middle Gila River in central Arizona constructed complex and extensive earthen irrigation systems during their prehistoric occupation (Haury 1976); in the Historic period, Akimel O'odham groups also utilized irrigation to water many of the same lands. More recent canals that traverse the area likewise would be expected to exhibit some of the same characteristics as their predecessors, although differences between modern and prehistoric canals will be discussed below. The pollen and micro-invertebrate assemblage and sediment signatures that characterize canal conditions in modern canals appear to have great value in reconstructing past canal conditions.

Earthen canals are presently uncommon in central and southern Arizona, and as they increasingly become lined with cement, opportunities to study them diminish (Figure 3). Although a number of fine synthetic studies have focused on prehistoric, protohistoric, and historical irrigation systems and communities (Doolittle 1990; Mabry 1996; Sheridan 1988), less work has been done with sediments and organisms contained within canals. We believe this study of modern canal analogs to be the first major study of its kind for the region.

Within the next decade, extensive archaeological excavations on GRIC lands will focus on understanding canal systems from main headgate to the smallest canal that diverts water onto a farmer's field. Investigators intend to examine both prehistoric Hohokam and historical Akimel O'odham canal systems occupying the same landscape but separated by centuries. Therefore, the primary goals of this project are to both guide future archaeological sampling of canals and provide interpretive perspective on canal sediment and biological organisms contained within them, via the following specific aims:

1. Summarize the literature of previous canal studies, highlighting the diversity of topics that have been explored with these data;

2. Compare and contrast modern pollen signatures and assemblages of micro-invertebrates (molluscs and ostracodes) associated with earthen canals and other local fluvial locations, and examine results for insights into the geographic scale of pollen contribution and the energy conditions of canals as reflected in organisms present;

3. Provide inventories of local vegetation to determine whether modern nearby vegetation registers in pollen spectra of fluvial locations and determine the presence of any nonlocal pollen that may have traveled long distances;

4. Evaluate whether variability exists in paired pollen or micro-invertebrate samples from the same sample loci, acknowledging that additional samples would be required to fully document the nature and extent of any variability;

5. Examine sediment traits of the samples for hydrological implications, as well as for information pertinent to predicting presence of pollen and micro-invertebrates;

6. Ascertain whether agricultural pollen occurs in canals, suggestive of the crops grown along an irrigation system;

7. Determine the nature of any useful information contained within clean-out sediment scraped from canal bottoms and deposited along canal levees;

8. Delineate the unique or complementary contributions of each dataset to canal studies, and provide guidance for archaeologists interested in sampling canal sediments.

The current SCIP (San Carlos Irrigation Project) canal system on GRIC lands was formally begun early in this century (Figure 4). It was essentially completed by the mid-1930s, except for some minor recent modifications (Pfaff 1994). The project includes the Florence–Casa Grande Canal and the Ashurst-Hayden Diversion Dam and is designed to irrigate 100,000 acres, though never has the maximum been irrigated in any given year (Pfaff 1994; Wilson 1999). As it exists today, the SCIP system (shown partially in Figure 4) includes a storage dam (Coolidge), one functioning diversion dam (Ashurst-Hayden), 500 miles of irrigation channels, and 98 irrigation wells (Pfaff 1996). The system also has a power component consisting of an unused hydroelectric plant at Coolidge Dam, 152 miles of transmission lines, and other components of a power system (Pfaff 1996). The SCIP canal system is currently scheduled to undergo major alteration, aimed at bringing significant additional acreage under irrigation.

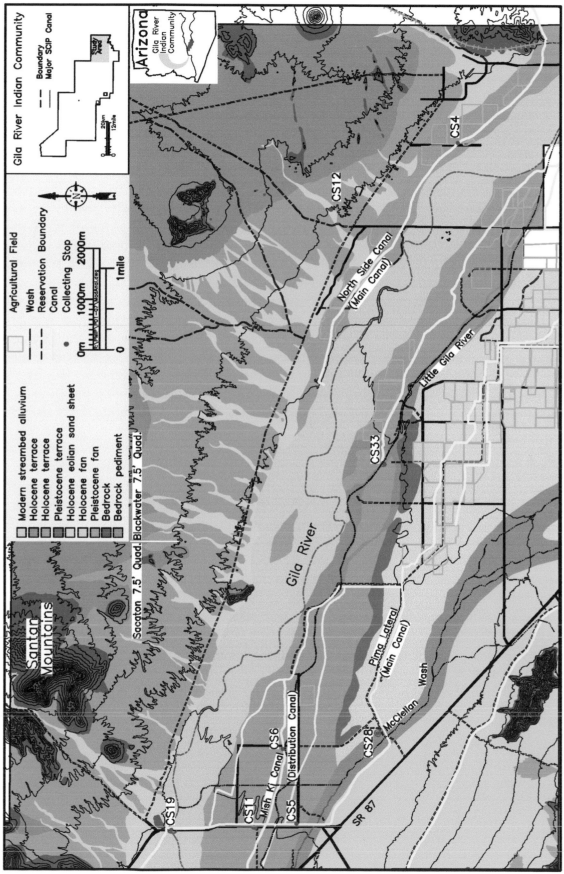

Figure 4. Portions of the USGS 7.5' Sacaton and Blackwater quadrangles showing surficial geomorphic landforms, major irrigation canals, and collecting stops

Differences clearly exist between modern SCIP and prehistoric Hohokam and historical Akimel O'odham irrigation systems, affecting the applicability of the modern analogs to past canal systems. First, canals are now so carefully maintained that few plants grow along the levees. Prehistorically, canalside vegetation could have included cottonwood, willow, reed grass (*Phragmites*), arrow-weed, and cattail, all plants favoring floodplain settings (Crown 1987). Pollen and macrobotanical studies have suggested that weedy cheno-ams, as well as agave and cholla, were encouraged or deliberately cultivated along canals (Gish 1989; Miksicek 1995; Smith 1995). As a result, some form of canalside vegetation removal or management was likely necessary, similar to that reported for the Historic period prior to the 1960s (Rea 1997). Second, today canalside vegetation is only rarely burned during the dry season. During the prehistoric Hohokam occupation, burning may have been a common method for removing plants that choked canals, resulting in burned plant parts being deposited into canal sediments. Third, the Gila River would have been the major water source in the past, while modern water sources for farmers may include one or more of the following: Gila River water diverted at the Ashurst-Hayden Dam, which could settle out upland, nonlocal pollen types; local wells; residual water from the San Carlos Irrigation Project system; and Central Arizona Project (CAP) water brought across the state from the Colorado River. Fourth, hydrological parameters differ, in that prehistoric Gila River flows would have been seasonally and annually variable, with high winter rain and springtime snowmelt flows, a period of low flow in late spring and early summer, and then moderate flow during midsummer monsoonal rains; today, flow in the irrigation systems is managed throughout the year to coincide with year-round agricultural needs. And finally, the distances that prehistoric canals carried water likely differed from those of modern canals. Most prehistoric main and distribution canals were probably shorter than modern canals of the same ranks.

In addition, considerable change has occurred along the middle Gila River within the last century, especially in relation to the Gila River floodplain and valley bottom (Rea 1983, 1997:62; Wilson 1999). Grasslands have been significantly reduced in extent, native species have been replaced by exotics, and some locales have been severely overgrazed (Rea 1997:50). Local groups once used fire regularly in grasslands to drive cotton rats and rabbits into the open as a form of communal hunting (Dobyns 1981; Rea 1997:45). Today, however, ground-blanketing, historically introduced plants such as red brome *(Bromus rubens)* carry fire into Sonoran Desert vegetation not adapted to burning (Rea 1997:58). Despite these changes and differences between ancient and modern canals and environments, an understanding of prehistoric Hohokam and historical Akimel O'odham irrigation systems along the Gila River will be facilitated by an understanding of modern earthen SCIP canals in the same environment.

Previous researchers have documented middle Gila River irrigation canal systems (Craig and Phillips 2001; Crown 1984, 1987; Gregory and Huckleberry 1994; Haury 1976; Midvale 1946, 1963; Mitalsky [Midvale 1935]; Woodbury 1961) and have reconstructed streamflow (Graybill et al. 1999). GRIC archaeologists have recently focused on geomorphological mapping of the middle Gila River valley (Waters 1996; Waters and Ravesloot 2000), detailed mapping of prehistoric Hohokam canal alignments and settlements in the Gila Butte–Snaketown region (Neily et al. 2000; Woodson and Davis 2001), and documentation of buried canal alignments associated with both the Gila River (Foster 2000; Woodson 2001a, 2001b; Woodson and Randolph 2000) and the Salt River (Woodson and Neily 1998). Nonirrigation agricultural systems are also of interest (Neily 1997; Neily et al. 1999; Woodson and Davis 2001; Woodson and Randolph 2000). Ultimately, these studies will contribute to an understanding of the relationships between landscape change, irrigation agriculture, and Hohokam cultural evolution (Waters and Ravesloot 2000, 2001; Woodson and Davis 2001). A research design for the study of prehistoric and historical irrigation systems on the agricultural lands of the middle Gila River valley is in preparation (Woodson 2002).

The alluvial history of the Gila River reported by geomorphologists provides an opportunity to examine landscape changes coincident with cultural changes (Huckleberry 1993; Waters and Ravesloot 2000, 2001) and helps place the study of irrigation systems within a geomorphological perspective. For the period between 18,000 and 4250–4400 cal yr B.P., the middle Gila River accumulated alluvium within a broad eroded channel (Waters and Ravesloot 2000). Then the river channel stabilized and began accumulating sediment from overbank flooding, until a particularly stable period between 500 and 200 cal yr B.P. when soil formed on the floodplain. Two periods of channel cutting and widening have been documented within this long sequence, the first at 800–950 cal yr B.P. and the second in the late nineteenth century A.D. All dates reported in this manuscript are presented as originally published.

At present, the earliest GRIC irrigation canal dates to 1765 ± 60 14C B.P., during a time of river channel stabilization (Waters and Ravesloot 2000:53). This was followed by over 1,000 years of canal system development and expansion. Increasing human occupation through the Colonial (A.D. 500–900) and Sedentary (A.D. 900–1100) periods ended during the Classic period (A.D. 1100–1450), when sites were abandoned and canals consolidated (Doyel 1979; Haury 1976; Wilcox 1979). The significant era of channel cutting and widening in the 800–950 cal yr B.P. pre-Classic to Classic period transition likely created major problems for Hohokam agriculturalists, while a similar situation in the late 1800s probably caused problems for Historic period irrigators (Dobyns 1981; Waters and Ravesloot 2000, 2001).

8

Previous Hohokam Canal Studies

Organisms and sediment have been examined from prehistoric Hohokam irrigation canals for over 20 years. At this point, it is appropriate to summarize what has been learned from pollen, larger plant remains, micro-invertebrates, and sedimentological data contained within canals, including an overview of the categories of information available from each dataset as well as insights gained on the seasons and mechanics of canal operation. Such a synthesis can help guide future GRIC studies of prehistoric canals.

Pollen

Numerous projects have included pollen analysis as a component of prehistoric canal research (Table 1), including some unpublished reports (Gish 1978, 1979a; Schoenwetter 1980) and reports on historical canals (Fish 1986). Bohrer (1970) was among the very first to examine pollen from ancient canal sediments. In an earlier review, Gish (1989:326–332) was the first to provide a regional perspective on pollen from Hohokam lateral and distribution canals along the Salt and New Rivers and from the Cave and Queen Creek areas. Since then, palynologists have analyzed more than 200 pollen samples from dozens of prehistoric Hohokam canals, including some from the middle Gila River (Smith 1997a; Woodson and Neily 1998). Canal pollen studies have contributed information to several research themes and questions summarized in the following sections and detailed in Table 1.

Thirty years of canal pollen studies have been accomplished with little direct information on how pollen assemblages arrive at, and become incorporated within, irrigation canals. Rather, in the Southwest, studies of noncanal alluvial locations have provided the analogs for interpretation of canal pollen assemblages. For example, pollen investigations of modern alluvium have revealed that pollen grains contained in water-deposited sediments arrive at deposition sites by a variety of vectors, including air, water, insects, and reworking of older sediments; each mechanism entails a separate suite of processes (Fall 1987; Hevly et al. 1965; Schoenwetter and Doerschlag 1971; Solomon et al. 1982). The complexity of pollen transport and deposition in water has also been studied in streams (Peck 1973; Pennington 1979; Starling and Crowder 1981) and by looking at hydraulic sorting of pollen by shape and size (Brush and Brush 1972; Davis and Brubaker 1973).

Insights from water control features such as canals, reservoirs, and drainage ditches are potentially diverse. For example, some have contained cultigen pollen considered to have originated in associated Hohokam fields (Fish 1987; Lytle-Webb 1981; McLaughlin 1976; Nials and Fish 1988), as has been the case elsewhere in the world (Puleston 1977; Wiseman 1983, 1990). Infusions of upland pollen types in canal waters can create unique signatures in downstream locations, helping document season of deposition and possibly discriminate water sources for multicatchment drainages (Fish 1998). Riparian plants such as cattails and sedges can be introduced into canals either by plants growing along canal perimeters or by their pollen being transported long distances in moving water (Fish 1998).

Table 1. Previous Studies of Pollen within Irrigation Canals

Site/Area	Time Period	Canal Rank or Size	Number of Pollen Samples and Canal Features	Other Canal-Related Contexts Sampled	Crop Pollen in Canal Samples	Major Conclusions	Reference
AZ:U:9:46/ Tempe	Classic		17 samples from 2 canals		*Zea mays,* cf. *Gossypium*	Canals contain both riverine and upland pollen types, suggestive of canal use.	Lytle-Webb 1981
Salt-Gila area, central Arizona	Classic		7 levee samples; 11 canal fill samples		*Zea mays, Cucurbita* sp. (wild or domestic)	Pollen in bank levee deposits is likely contemporary with active canal use; pollen in fill documents conditions after canal use; pollen and macrofossils, coupled with ecology, suggest some burning of canal-clogging weeds and nearby fields.	Bohrer 1992; Fish 1983; Miksicek 1983

Larger Plant Remains (Macrofossils, Flotation Samples)

Examination of larger plant parts, either as macrofossils or from within flotation samples, is best represented by the works of Miksicek (1983, 1987, 1989, 1995). Hundreds of samples examined from canals and reservoirs have contained wood charcoal, evidence of domesticates and wild plants, and algal spores. Combined with other evidence, these data have permitted a variety of interpretations. For example, the relatively high proportion of upland charcoal within canals, including juniper (*Juniperus* sp.), pine (*Pinus* sp.), and oak (*Quercus* sp.), has been interpreted as a result of ancient flooding, while the presence of certain halophytes such as inkweed (*Sueda* sp.) and iodine bush (*Allenrolfea* sp.) imply more saline (arid) situations (Miksicek 1989). Burned grass evidence from near a canal in the Queen Creek area contributed to a story of agricultural field maintenance by use of fire (Bohrer 1992; Miksicek 1983). Like pollen, the record of larger plant parts has also been used to suggest seasonality of canal use when the canals incorporate plant parts available within relatively brief periods of the calendar year (Miksicek 1989).

Micro-invertebrates (Molluscs and Ostracodes)

Molluscs are micro-invertebrates that include both gastropods (snails) and pelecypods (clams). Gastropods may live in both terrestrial and aquatic systems, whereas pelecypods are found only in water. Molluscs form a calcium carbonate exoskeleton (shell) of aragonite, calcite, or both (Bequaert and Miller 1973) that is frequently preserved in the archaeological record. Molluscs in irrigation canals are primarily indicative of aquatic conditions; however, it is not uncommon to find terrestrial forms in the terminal stages of canal desiccation.

Ostracodes are also micro-invertebrates, having a two-valve calcite carapace (shell) that also is preserved in the archaeological record. The shell may be smooth or elaborately ornamented, with ornamentation affected by environmental conditions (Pokorný 1978). Ostracodes can inhabit a wide range of water chemistry, from freshwater to alkali-rich or calcium-rich saline waters (Palacios-Fest et al. 1994).

Elsewhere in the world, ostracodes have been used as indicators of agricultural activity, such as by the pre-Hispanic Maya in Belize (Bradbury et al. 1987). Other studies have also shown the relation between ostracodes and agricultural activities over long intervals of prehistory (Curtis et al. 1995; Goman and Byrne 1998). However, these latter studies compare ostracodes from lake deposits with pollen grains of cultigens to infer environmental changes. None of these studies established a direct connection between irrigation canal operation and ostracode populations. In the Hohokam region, environmental reconstructions have all been made assuming that the species recovered in prehistoric canals share the ecological requirements of their modern counterparts known from lakes, ponds, and streams.

Aquatic molluscs and ostracodes are sensitive to water parameters such as temperature, pH, salinity, alkalinity, and ions. Changes in these parameters are a major factor controlling presence/absence, population size, diversity, and some intraspecific variations. Because the ecological requirements of many species are known (Bequaert and Miller 1973; Delorme 1969, 1989; Forester 1991), these organisms are an excellent proxy for environmental reconstructions within canal systems (Table 2). Varying length of organism life cycles (for example, in ostracodes ranging from four weeks to six months) enables the determination of longevity of canal operation and seasonality. Given the known temperature and salinity tolerances of particular species, investigators can infer during which time of year a specific canal or canal segment may have been active in the past.

The earliest studies of micro-invertebrates in the Hohokam region occurred decades ago (Antevs 1941; Barber 1984; Haury1937). More recently, Miksicek (1985, 1987, 1995) and Vokes and Miksicek (1987) were the first to use molluscs to understand the effects of water flow and humidity and to evaluate the impact of human activity on the environment in central Arizona. The study of ostracodes within prehistoric canals, pioneered by Palacios-Fest (1989), provided insights into the influence of water salinity and temperature (Palacios-Fest 1994, 1997a, 1997c; Woodson and Neily 1998). The same author conducted the first attempt to combine ostracode and mollusc analysis to decipher the environmental signal from multiple organism groups (Palacios-Fest 1997b).

Sediment Studies

Important information contained within prehistoric canals has also come from studies of their sediment. For example, particle size is often utilized as a proxy for water velocity (Huckleberry 1999), assuming that larger sand grains are deposited during episodes of faster flowing water and that silts and clays settle out when water velocity slows or water is stagnant. Several pollen analysts have demonstrated that the composition of canal pollen assemblages correlates to sediment texture, which is a function of flow regimes (Fish 1987; Gish 1989). Smith (1995) showed a statistical relationship between pollen abundance and sediment texture, which served as a proxy to interpret flow regimes. Sediment analysis provides an objective measure of alluvial texture; in this study the analysis of sediment deposition will form the basis of a comparative sedimentological database for canal systems along the middle Gila River.

Insights from Previous Irrigation Canal Studies

Archaeologists have used data recorded during previous studies of irrigation canals to explore a diversity of topics relevant to ancient irrigation in the Hohokam region. These topics range from the evolution of irrigation technology to the signatures that distinguish

Site/Area	Time Period	Remarks	Reference
Las Acequias-Los Muertos/Tempe	Pioneer/Classic		Vokes and Miksicek 1987
La Cuenca del Sedimento/Tempe	Pioneer/Classic		Miksicek 1989
Las Acequias/Tempe	Pioneer/Classic	...odes from irrigation	Palacios-Fest 1989
Las Acequias/Tempe	Pioneer/Classic	...tracode shell ...gation canals to ...natic trends.	Palacios-Fest 1994
Las Acequias/Tempe	Pioneer/Classic	... ostracode shell ...itical coefficients to ...re.	Palacios-Fest 1997a
McDowell-to-Shea sites/Scottsdale	Sedentary/Class		Miksicek 1995
Pueblo Blanco/Tempe	Classic	...phic study of ...igation canals.	Palacios-Fest 1995; 1997c
McDowell-to-Shea sites/Scottsdale	Sedentary/Class		Palacios-Fest 1996a
La Cuenca del Sedimento/Tempe			Palacios-Fest 1997d
AZ U:15:282/ Pueblo Blanco area		...for an environmental	Palacios-Fest 1997e
Phoenix (no site available)			Palacios-Fest 1997f
Pecos Road/Chandler	Sedentary/Clas	...ine the signals of ...lluscs.	Palacios-Fest 1997b
Organ Pipe National Monument		...codes from Hohokam	Palacios-Fest 1999b
Las Capas/Tucson	San Pedro pha... agricultural pe...	...-Hohokam canal	Palacios-Fest 1999a Palacios-Fest et al. 2001

water-related features from other cultural loci, and include a variety of insights into canal construction and operation. This literature is summarized below.

Evolution of Irrigation Technology/Canal Construction

Researchers have previously speculated how and when people began to control water input into canals, and a recent study revealed that microfossils are capable of reflecting changing water management practices in prehistory. Palacios-Fest and colleagues (Palacios-Fest 1999a; Palacios-Fest et al. 2001) relied upon ostracodes as indicators of modes of water control for agriculture in the middle Santa Cruz valley in southern Arizona. They documented how San Pedro phase farmers at the Las Capas site made the transition from opportunistic to functional canal operation between 3000 and 2400 B.P. During early canal operations, agriculturalists were subject to monsoonal rains, hence their fields were flooded during late summer storm flows. As people learned how to control water input, they changed to a functional canal operation that allowed deliberate water control from permanent streams. Variations in ostracode populations at Las Capas suggest alternating intervals of salinization and water input consistent with episodes of headgate opening and closing. A consequence of gaining control over water was an increase in maize production that archaeologists associate with increasing population at the site. Ostracode paleoecology suggests that the Santa Cruz River floodplain was subject to human impact via cycles of water input, a scenario proposed previously by Waters (1988).

Information about canal construction has primarily been based on field geomorphology of excavated features (Howard and Huckleberry 1991; Huckleberry 1993) and on modeling canal systems (Howard 1990). A record of postholes reveals that posts were often placed within canal channels to serve as temporary supports for brush, basketry, and other materials to slow water flow (Ackerly et al. 1989:183). At Los Muertos, a Hohokam site within the Las Acequias canal system, pollen analysis suggested that grass (Poaceae) and cattail (*Typha* sp.) were likely parts of a brush baffle construction (Gish 1989). In some cases, pollen may be all that remains of the organic resources used to help slow or direct water flow within a system. At Cave Buttes along Cave Creek, high cheno-am values were interpreted as evidence of ground disturbance associated with canal construction and agriculture (Gish 1979b).

Canal Operation/Flow Regimes

Distance from Source Intakes

Changes in pollen spectra have been interpreted to relate to canal rank, size, and distance from headwaters. Homogenized pollen assemblages are associated with main canals (Fish 1987; Smith 1995), and smaller canals are characterized by more local (Sonoran

14

Desert) pollen types (Gish 1989). In the Las Acequias canal system, Gish (1989:301–303) compared pine pollen percentages to sediment texture, canal rank, and canal size and showed that the relative amounts of pine pollen decreased as distance from canal headwaters increased and as canal rank decreased. The study focused on basal canal sediments interpreted to represent first use/filling of canals, rather than on the midchannel fill, which is frequently the focus of canal studies. The highest percentages of pine pollen were associated with silt and clay sediments in main canals and at sites closest to the river. Las Acequias distribution and lateral canals distant from the river were characterized by higher percentages of cheno-am pollen, which Gish (1989:303) interpreted to reflect local vegetation.

Canal Operation/Maintenance

A number of studies have focused on aspects of canal operation. For example, molluscs have been used to interpret long-term episodes of canal desiccation and standing water (Miksicek 1995; Vokes and Miksicek 1987) that imply closed headgates or some other reason for the unavailability of flowing water. Ostracodes have also been used to suggest alternating episodes of water salinization and freshening (Palacios-Fest 1996a). Palacios-Fest (1997b) found that both ostracodes and molluscs together were helpful in reconstructing periods of flowing or stagnant waters in the middle Gila River valley. The presence of *Cyprideis beaconensis* (a salt-tolerant species not common when salinity is low) in irrigation canals at a Phoenix site (Palacios-Fest 1997f) indicates that these canals became highly saline.

Variation in ostracode assemblages exhibits significant changes from sample to sample within individual Pueblo Blanco canals, suggesting a pattern of canal water salinization and dilution (Palacios-Fest 1995). Progressive salinization of canal waters resulted from gradual evaporation after the initial filling of canals, a process interpreted as anthropogenic rather than climatic in origin for two reasons. First, the cycling occurred in a relatively short time, if it can be assumed that the canal strata represent the last irrigation cycle for the particular canal. Second, the pattern consistently recorded two evaporative cycles that suggest different episodes of canal operation.

Pollen analyses from Hohokam canals in the Phoenix Basin have also contributed some insights into canal operation and maintenance. Sediment texture and pollen abundance correspond to flow regimes (this report; Smith 1995). Sedimentological data and high percentages of pine pollen associated with silts and clays were considered indicative of water-saturated conditions and long-term flows in a Las Colinas canal (Nials and Fish 1988). Cattail pollen in Scottsdale system canals was interpreted to reflect slow or stagnant water conditions, such as in a pool that became isolated as the system emptied (Smith 1995).

Canal clean-out sediments would be expected to contain a diversity of waterborne pollen types in addition to pollen from weedy plants growing along canal berms. Levee samples from various projects (Fish 1981, 1983; Gish 1985) had high percentages of spiderling (*Boerhaavia* sp.), globe mallow (*Sphaeralcea* sp.), wild buckwheat (*Eriogonum* sp.), and other weeds (potentially highly productive plants of disturbed habitats) considered likely to be contemporaneous with active canal use and reflective of a disturbed, mesic environment. Pollen from within canal fill, by contrast, more likely documents conditions after canal abandonment (Fish 1983).

At the Las Colinas site in the Phoenix Basin, pollen studies combined with sedimentological data were used to interpret burning of organic materials within a canal as a form of canal maintenance (Nials and Fish 1988). In the Queen Creek area, Bohrer (1992) suggested that charred grass remains and other burned materials inside canals, and fluctuating pollen frequencies of various plants, reflect both canal maintenance and the burning of field stubble. An alternative opinion on the use of fire in prehistoric Sonoran Desert ecosystems has been suggested by Fish (1997, 2000), who considers anthropogenic fires, for whatever reasons, to have been of fairly limited extent.

Seasonality of Canal Operation

Palacios-Fest (1997a, 1997c) suggested that ostracodes and ostracode shell chemistry may be used to recognize seasonality of canal operation. For example, one study (Palacios-Fest 1997a) calculated water temperature based upon the Mg/Ca ratios of the ostracode shells. These findings suggest that water temperature at the time of shell formation was close to the minimum values recorded for the Phoenix Basin for the last 145 years. Ostracodes molt their skeletons between midnight and dawn, as do other invertebrates. The trend toward low temperatures shows that this molting process occurred mainly between late winter and early summer. Another study, using ostracode paleoecology only, indicates that the faunal associations responded to temperature and salinity (Palacios-Fest 1997c). In the first study it was possible to suggest specific temperatures, while the second study provides only a relative interpretation.

Several pollen analysts have attempted to infer the seasons during which Hohokam canals carried water, based on empirical studies that show a seasonal correspondence between pollen in the air and water samples from rivers and streams (Bonny 1978; Crowder and Cuddy 1973; Peck 1973; Pennington 1979; Starling and Crowder 1981). Spring canal flows have been interpreted from enhanced alder (*Alnus* sp.) and juniper pollen (Fish 1987:166; Gish 1988, 1989; McLaughlin 1976; Smith 1995). Fish (1987) and Nials and Fish (1988) considered local, summer weed and agricultural pollen to suggest summer flows in canals. Gish (1989:309) used pollen data to interpret spring and summer use of Las Acequias main and distribution canals, in addition to summer use of small, feeder canals. Enhanced pine and oak values from canal samples have been interpreted as complementary early summer signals because both trees are pollinating from May through June (Fish 1987; Gish 1989). Therefore, the combined interpretation of pollen records and ostracode shell chemistry are significantly consistent with respect to the seasonality of canal operation.

<u>Crops in Field Systems/Encouragement of Plants along Canals</u>

Maize (*Zea* sp.), cotton (*Gossypium* sp.), and squash (*Cucurbita* sp.) pollen have all been recovered from canal sediments, with crop pollen usually more frequent in the small canals supplying fields (Fish 1987; Gish 1989). Attempts to determine which crops were grown in field systems should therefore focus on the smaller canals and possible field areas in the vicinity of feeder canals. Pollen and macrobotanical studies have shown that wild plants, such as cheno-ams, agave (*Agave* sp.), and cholla (*Cylindropuntia* sp.), were probably encouraged or deliberately cultivated along canals (Gish 1989; Miksicek 1995; Smith 1995). Possibly these plants were also in nearby agricultural fields, or in the case of agave and cholla, along the edges of fields in the Lehi Terrace system (Gish 1989; Miksicek 1989). Maize pollen at Las Colinas (Fish 1981) was present only in the basal canal samples, consistent with an interpretation of accumulation with the final use of the canal.

Canal Capacity or Rank within a Prehistoric Irrigation System

The micro-invertebrate record reveals that canals dominated by *Ilyocypris bradyi* are usually main canals; those dominated by *Candona patzcuaro* and *Herpetocypris brevicaudata* or others are commonly distribution canals; and those dominated by *Cypridopsis vidua* and *Limnocythere staplini* are more likely lateral canals (Palacios-Fest 1997c). However, it is unclear whether this pattern is related to canal rank, desiccation processes, or possibly some other factor. Additional study of canal systems might help clarify the issue, coupling micro-invertebrates and archaeological evidence, to assess the rank of ancient canals within systems. In terms of pollen studies, main canals produce the most general pollen spectra, with pollen specificity increasing with decreasing canal rank (Fish 1987; Gish 1989; Smith 1995).

Irrigation Technology through Time

Hohokam irrigation technology has a surprising time depth, with engineering becoming increasingly sophisticated through the Hohokam occupation. Canals examined for micro-invertebrates represent a broad range of temporal associations, from the earliest San Pedro phase formalized canals (Palacios-Fest 1996b; Palacios-Fest et al. 2001) to the Classic period canals at Pueblo Blanco (Palacios-Fest 1995, 1997c). Most studies have included canals representing agricultural activity from the pre-Classic through the Classic period, though the bulk of the work has been done on Classic period canals. Because of the relatively small number of micro-invertebrate studies that have been completed, and because the projects they represent cover broad expanses of time, it is difficult to determine any patterns that are time-related (for example, how canal operation might have differed between the pre-Classic and the Classic period). This same situation essentially exists for the pollen record as well. One major contribution of the GRIC canal system excavations would be to acquire adequate samples clearly representing various phases of the prehistoric chronological sequence, so that analysts can determine potential trends in canal use through time.

Water Storage in Reservoirs/Clay Settling Basin

Reservoirs have yielded evidence of long-term water storage. Bayman and colleagues (1997) studied a small reservoir in the Picacho Basin in search of ostracodes, but none were found. However, the presence of pondweed (*Lemna* sp.) revealed that this site was indeed a reservoir that had held water for long periods of time. Elsewhere, in Organ Pipe National Monument, Palacios-Fest (1999b) reported a monospecific population of *Heterocypris antilliensis* in a sediment deposit measuring 2 m thick; the occurrence of this species suggests that the reservoir contained water for a long time. Some reservoirs appear to have been fed by rainwater only when the Hohokam dammed small seeps to keep water permanently available along their trade routes (Palacios-Fest 1999b). Other reservoirs contain evidence of intake canals. One feature originally considered to be a reservoir was reinterpreted as a clay settling basin after analysts assessed fine-interval samples of pollen and physical sediment data, where repetitive sequences of fill-cycle sediments were associated with repeating patterns of high pine pollen percentages in the top clay layers (Nials and Fish 1988).

Differentiating Irrigation Features from Other Cultural Features

Features may be difficult to interpret in the field because of limited excavation data or factors that obscure cultural features over long periods of time. The use of both micro-invertebrates and pollen can assist in these cases. The very occurrence of micro-invertebrates suggests that water was once present in a feature (Palacios-Fest 1997b). Most palynologists have identified a pollen signature unique to canals, composed of riparian species and pine and juniper percentages higher than those typically found in Sonoran Desert soils and archaeological contexts such as middens or pits of various types (Fish 1981). Enhanced pollen values of pine, other upland plants, and riparian species are generally interpreted to reflect water-deposited sediments (Fish 1987; Gish 1984, 1989; Lytle-Webb 1981; Smith 1995). In one case, the pollen data revealed that two channels in a main canal were prehistoric, as analysts identified no pollen from plant taxa introduced during the Historic period or more recently (Gish 1988). In another case, higher representation of weed types was considered to be a characteristic distinguishing canals from other cultural features (Gish 1985).

Climate Change

Palacios-Fest (1994) was the first researcher to incorporate ostracode shell chemistry analysis into the examination of past climate change, using three ostracode species

18

(*Limnocythere staplini, Cypridopsis vidua,* and *Candona patzcuaro*). All three species showed similar trends, although each indicated different chemical composition. These trends were consistent with periods of climatic change, including a couple of flood events and a general increase in temperature between the 1200s and the 1450s (Palacios-Fest 1994).

Synthesis of Canal Insights

It is clear that plant and micro-invertebrate remains contained within canal sediments, coupled with sedimentological analysis, can provide information on a range of topics related to irrigation agriculture (Table 3). In some cases, micro-invertebrates alone provide insights, such as on the evolution of irrigation technology and on aspects of climatic change suggested by flood events or temperature trends. In other cases, pollen and larger plant remains offer unique perspectives, such as on aspects of canal construction components, distance of canal segments from river headwaters, burning of vegetation as a form of canal maintenance, the nature of crops grown in agricultural fields, and the encouragement of wild plants along canals and the edges of nearby fields. Complementary analyses of micro-invertebrates and pollen and other plant remains have revealed episodes of water flow in canals versus periods of water stagnation or desiccation, have provided insight into seasonality of canal operation, and have proved useful in understanding long-term water storage in reservoirs. Micro-invertebrate and pollen data are also useful in distinguishing main, distribution, and lateral canals, although more work is needed to clarify why micro-invertebrate signatures vary among canal ranks. Both datasets can help differentiate irrigation from other cultural features. Regarding temporal trends, too few studies have been accomplished on micro-invertebrates and pollen to permit the documentation of clear-cut differences between pre-Classic and Classic period canals.

Table 3. Summarized Insights from Past Studies of Pollen and Micro-invertebrates within Irrigation Canals and Associated Features

Topic of Study	Data Set(s)	Insights	References
Evolution of irrigation technology/ canal construction	Ostracodes	It was possible to distinguish the transition from an opportunistic (less-managed) to a functional (more managed) mode of canal operation 3000-2400 B.P.	Palacios-Fest 1999a; Palacios-Fest el al. 2001; Waters 1988
	Pollen	Grass and cattails were part of brush baffle construction.	Gish 1979b, 1989
Canal operation/flow regimes			
A. Distance from source intakes	Pollen	Pine pollen percentages and sediment texture can serve as a general gauge of distance from the canal headwaters.	Fish 1987; Gish 1989; Smith 1995
B. Canal operation/maintenance	Molluscs and ostracodes	Micro-invertebrates reveal episodes of dessication and standing water, suggesting closed headgates, periods of flowing or stagnant waters, and patterns of canal salinization and dilution.	Miksicek 1995; Palacios-Fest 1995, 1996a, 1997b, 1997f; Vokes and Miksicek 1987
	Pollen	Sediment and pollen data can indicate long-term flows. Pollen abundance and sediment texture correspond to canal flow regimes. Cattail pollen can signify slow or stagnant water. Canal clean-out sediments along levees contain a diversity of water borne pollen types, along with pollen from weedy plants growing along canals.	Fish 1981, 1983; Gish 1985; Nials and Fish 1988; Smith 1995
	Pollen and macrofossils	Canal clogging vegetation was likely burned as routine canal maintenance. Agricultural fields were also burned to prepare for planting.	Bohrer 1992; Fish 1997, 2000; Nials and Fish 1988
C. Seasonality of canal operation	Ostracodes and ostracode shell chemistry	Ostracodes occupied canals between late winter and early summer. Another study suggested relative temperatures.	Palacios-Fest 1997a, 1997c
	Pollen	Spring and summer flows have been interpreted from specific pollen spectra.	Fish 1987; Gish 1988, 1989; McLaughlin 1976; Nials and Fish 1988; Smith 1995
D. Cultivation/encouragement of plants along canals	Pollen and macrofossils	Maize, cotton, and squash pollen were recovered in canal sediments. Wild plants (for example cheno-ams, agave, cholla) were likely encouraged along canals or along the edges of nearby agricultural fields.	Fish 1981, 1987; Gish 1989; Miksicek 1989, 1995; Smith 1995
Canal capacity/rank within an irrigation system	Ostracodes	Different ostracodes possibly represent main vs. distribution vs. lateral canals. More work is needed.	Palacios-Fest 1997c
	Pollen	Main canals produced the most general pollen spectra, with pollen specificity increasing with decreasing canal rank. Crop pollen was highest from smaller canals.	Fish 1987; Gish 1989; Smith 1995
Irrigation technology through time	Ostracodes and molluscs	Too few studies to determine any patterns related to pre-Classic vs. Classic periods. Also, it is hard to date canals.	Palacios-Fest 1995, 1996b, 1997c; Palacios-Fest et al. 2001
Water storage: reservoirs, clay basins	Macrofossils	Macrofossils revealed that a reservoir held water for long periods.	Bayman et al. 1997
	Ostracodes	Ostracodes also revealed that a reservoir held water for a long time. Water may have been kept permanently available along trade routes.	Palacios-Fest 1996b
	Pollen	Some features were more likely pottery clay settling basins, rather than water storage reservoirs.	Nials and Fish 1988
Differentiating irrigation features from cultural features	Ostracodes and molluscs	Their very presence suggests water presence in the past.	Palacios-Fest 1997b
	Pollen	Riparian and high pine pollen values can help differentiate water control features, as does sediment texture.	Fish 1981, 1987; Gish 1984, 1985, 1988, 1989; Lytle-Webb 1981; Smith 1995
Climate change	Ostracode shell chemistry	Ostracode shell chemistry was used to suggest periods of climatic change, including flood events and increasing temperature between the A.D. 1200s and 1450s.temperature between the A.D. 1200s and 1450s.	Palacios-Fest 1994

MATERIALS AND METHODS

For this study, analysts examined canal sediments sampled from pits dug within three winter-dormant earthen-lined canals between late November 1998 and late January 1999. Additional mesic locations sampled include surface floodplain sediments of the Gila and Little Gila rivers and an ephemeral wash on a Holocene fan located some distance above the Gila River floodplain. These noncanal sites provide perspective on locations experiencing alternating wet and dry conditions, with prolonged periods of aridity, and serve as controls for the irrigation canal sediments. All locations are in the Blackwater and Sacaton quadrangles of the southeastern portion of GRIC lands (Figure 4).

Collecting Stations

The eight separate sampling loci or collecting stations (CS) discussed here were chosen to represent some of the diversity of locations present within an irrigation system as well as other mesic locations chosen for comparison. The collecting stations include three earthen canals, a canal clean-out, an ephemeral drainage across a Holocene fan where crops may have been grown with managed water diversion during rains, and three modern alluvial floodplain or wash locations, for a comparative perspective (Table 4). The three earthen canals sampled for this project are the Northside (CS4), Pima Lateral (CS5), and Mish Ki (CS6) canals (Table 5). The Gila River is diverted into the Florence–Casa Grande Canal at Ashurst-Hayden Dam, which feeds the Northside and Pima Lateral canals. These two canals then deliver water to smaller canals that in turn divert water to even smaller farm field ditches. Mish Ki Canal receives water from the Pima Lateral, then delivers it to smaller ditches. None of these three canals delivers water directly to fields. In terminology commonly utilized to describe the different types of prehistoric canals (Ackerly et al. 1987; Howard 1990; Masse 1991), the Pima Lateral and Northside canals would be considered main canals, whereas the Mish Ki Canal would be described as a distribution canal (Table 6).

The three canals vary in their distance from the Gila River, which provides the primary water source, along with groundwater (via wells) and CAP (Central Arizona Project) water, via the Pima Lateral Canal. Groundwater can account for between 2% and 100% of the total water supplied via these canals, though the use is often more limited, for example, not rising over 20% for the period 1982–1992 (SCIP Annual Irrigation Reports). Usage of CAP water is generally reserved for severe drought conditions. Although water was not flowing when the canal bottoms were sampled, during the period of this study the amount of water present in other parts of the canal system consisted of 50% or more natural river flows (in December 1998, 88% of the 3,694 acre feet of irrigation water came from natural flows; in January 1999, natural flows constituted 50% of the 3,710 acre feet of irrigation water [SCIP Annual Irrigation Reports]). Up to 60% of all the Gila River water diverted through the Florence–Casa Grande canal system can be lost to seepage, evaporation, and other factors.

Table 4. Collecting Stations Discussed in This Report

Collection Station	Samples	General Location	Landform	Quadrangle	Elevation	Date	Notes
CS4	9,10,11,12,13	Northside Canal	Canal within T-2 Terrace	Blackwater	1380'	11-23-98	Cottonfield also sampled
CS5	14,15,16	Pima Lateral Canal	Canal within T-2 Terrace	Sacaton	1305'	11-23-98	Old agricultural field nearby
CS6	17,18,19	Mish ki Canal	Canal within T-2 Terrace	Sacaton	1310'	11-23-98	Roadsides dominated by *Prosopis sp*
CS11	25,26	Canal clean out, Olberg Rd.		Sacaton	1300'	12-01-98	Canal clean-out samples
CS12	27,28	Holocene fan, Twin Buttes	Ephemeral drainage	Blackwater	1400'	12-17-98	Active drainage bottom & islands
CS19	42,43	Gila River Floodplain	Holocene alluvium	Sacaton	1290'	01-08-99	Below Olberg Bridge
CS28	60,61	McClellan Wash	Holocene alluvium	Sacaton	1310'	01-27-99	Grassy area, road to Hashani Kehk
CS33	70,71	Little Gila River	Holocene alluvium	Blackwater	1345'	01-27-99	Near Blackwater community

Abbreviations: CS = Collection Station

Table 5. Traits of Modern Canals Examined in this Study

	Canal type or rank[a]	Primary water source	Distance from head (Gila River)	Distance from Diversion	Shape of canal	Cross-sectional area[b]
Northside Canal (CS 4)	Main canal	Gila River	29 km (18 miles)	23.3 km (14.5 miles) from Florence-Casa Grande Canal	Parabolic	2 m^2
Pima Lateral Canal (CS 5)	Main canal	Gila River	54 km (33.5 miles)	31.4 km (19.5 miles) from Florence-Casa Grande Canal	Parabolic	9 m^2
Mish Ki Canal (CS 6)	Distribution canal	Gila River	53 km (33 miles)	4.8 km (3 miles) from Pima Lateral canal	Trapezoidal	3.4 m^2

[a]Terminology applied to prehistoric canal ranks. See text for further discussion.

[b] For parabolic canals, the calculation is $A = 2/3$ $(w \times d)$, where w = width of canal at water level, and d = maximum depth of water (estimated at 3/4 total depth). For trapezoidal canals, the calculation is $A = bd + Zd2$, where b = width of base of canal (where it is flat), d = maximum depth of water (estimated at 3/4 depth), and $Z = e/d$ (e = width of canal from edge to where the base becomes flat).

24

Table 6. Rank and Function of Prehistoric versus Modern Canals

Modern Rank	Modern Function	Prehistoric Rank	Prehistoric Function
Canal	Large delivery channel that delivers water to a smaller delivery channel	Main canal	Carries water from source to general vicinity of fields
Lateral canal and carry ditch	Delivers water to a carry ditch or directly to an on-farm field ditch	Distribution canal	Diverges from main canals and carries water to field area
Field ditch	Delivers water directly to fields	Lateral canal or field lateral canal	Transports water from a distribution or main canal into fields

The canals vary in cross-sectional area, calculated using the width and depth of the estimated water levels in each canal when two-thirds full. They also differ in shape from parabolic to trapezoidal. When modern canals are cleaned out they are generally trapezoidal, and as they accumulate sediments they become more parabolic (as are most prehistoric canals). The rate and amount of sediment deposition is dependent on factors such as water velocity, sediment particle size, and other channel traits.

Floodplain deposits of the Gila River (CS19), Little Gila River (CS33), McClellan Wash (CS28), and an ephemeral wash within a Holocene fan (CS12) were also included in this study (Table 4). Also, a dry canal along Olberg Road (CS11) yielded some recent canal clean-out debris representing sediment scraped from the canal bottom and sides and deposited on the side berms. Analysts intended to establish pollen profiles for these drier environments and to evaluate whether micro-invertebrates were routinely preserved in these deposits.

Nature of Samples

Pollen, micro-invertebrate (mollusc and ostracode), and sediment samples were excavated from still-wet canal bottoms, when canals were temporarily drained for maintenance between November and January. Up to five separate samples from a single pit within each canal represented sediment layers that appeared different in color and texture. Some samples, composed of dark sediment considered highly organic in content, were termed "black muck" samples. At floodplain locations, two separate samples consisting of small pinches of surface sediment were collected over a broad area to permit analysis of the nature of pollen and micro-invertebrate variability over short distances. To reduce the chance for overrepresentation of single pollen types, field personnel avoided sampling directly under plants. Wintertime sampling, when the majority of plants are dormant, offers a more average view of pollen deposited throughout previous growing seasons. This is a preliminary study designed to assess the feasibility of using modern canal analog data in archaeological reconstruction; thus, the low number of samples examined for each collecting station does not provide a statistically valid assessment of variability, and additional work would be needed to establish adequate sampling levels for different landforms, soil types, archaeological contexts, or sampling techniques.

Associated Plants

During the relatively dry winter of 1998/1999, the field personnel also made observations regarding plant distribution and seasonality at each collecting station to assess the influx of pollen of local plants into canals, in comparison to waterborne or broadly regional airborne pollen types. The first task was to walk over a broad area at least 1,000 square meters in size, list all plants present, and collect herbarium specimens. Observations included a subjective assessment of the role of each plant at the location, for example, whether the plant was dominant, co-dominant, common, sparse, or rare. Dominant and co-dominant taxa were those most obvious on the landscape in terms of numbers or size; usually woody trees or shrubs were the dominants, but at times herbaceous plants merited that distinction. Plants were considered common when at least 25 individuals were present, sparse when 11–24 were noted, and rare when 10 or less were seen. Another set of observations included flowering and fruiting of each taxon. Wind-pollinated plants in flower could possibly contribute pollen to the atmosphere during sampling and become incorporated in the study. Fruiting data were gathered for future interpretations of what resources local landforms have to offer humans at different times within a calendar year. For these observations, plants of each taxon were observed for whether their flowers were in bud, in full flower, wilted, or not present, and for the presence of immature fruit, mature fruit, or no fruit.

Laboratory Procedures

Pollen

For the 20 pollen samples derived from the collecting stations, subsamples (20 cc volume) from the sample bags were spiked with a known concentration (25,084 grains) of exotic spores (*Lycopodium*) to allow pollen concentration calculations. Pollen extraction steps included overnight hydrochloric and hydrofluoric acid treatments, followed by a density separation in zinc bromide (1.9 specific gravity). Pollen assemblages were identified by counting slide transects at 400x magnification to a 200-grain pollen sum, then scanning the entire slide at 100x magnification to record additional taxa. Aggregates (clumps of the same taxon) were counted as one grain per occurrence, and the taxon and size were recorded separately. Pollen aggregates are assumed to reflect deposition of flower anthers, which in terrestrial contexts signifies actual taxon presence (Gish 1991). In fluvial environments aggregates should be associated with higher-energy water flows because the clumps are heavier than single grains. Aggregates in fluvial sediments could also represent local vegetation growing in terrestrial environments (Gish 1991) along channel edges.

The absolute abundance of pollen contained in each sample (pollen concentration) is expressed as the number of pollen grains per cubic centimeter of sample sediment. Concentrations are used to investigate any sediment textural control on pollen abundance and are estimated by dividing the sample pollen count by the number of tracer spores counted. This result is multiplied by the tracer concentration, and the product is divided by the sample volume. Pollen percentages were also calculated: percentages normalize sample counts to 100, so that each taxon is expressed as a proportion of the sample pollen sum ([taxon count/sample pollen sum]×100).

Molluscs and Ostracodes

This study reports the results of 17 sediment samples processed for presence of molluscs and ostracodes. The analysis was designed to establish faunal associations present today within the SCIP canals and other fluvial locations on GRIC lands. Analysts then defined separate mollusc and ostracode assemblages with implications for hydrological conditions, based on known ecological information. These mollusc and ostracode signatures, when combined with sediment particle size analysis and indicator species data, will assist in the interpretation of past streamflow conditions in the canals. Because the canals and other locations were not flowing at the time of sampling, field personnel were unable to collect data on physical parameters (water temperature, pH, conductivity, major and minor ions, streamflow velocity) critical for assessing seasonality of assemblage formation. These seasonality assessments are planned for future studies.

Sediment samples were processed according to Forester's (1991) freeze-thaw technique modified by Palacios-Fest (1994). Sediment residuals were examined under a low-power stereoscopic microscope. Analysts determined faunal composition through routine study of samples and recorded total and relative abundance as well as standard taphonomic parameters—including fragmentation, disarticulation, abrasion, and adult/juvenile ratios (Delorme 1969)—to establish the synecology (ecology of the communities) as opposed to the autoecology (ecology of single species) of the canals. However, to integrate the environmental framework, single species ecology is reported in this study. Molluscs were picked and placed in a 55 ml Petri dish or on a micropaleontological slide. Ostracodes were picked and placed on micropaleontological slides.

The taphonomic features (listed above) observed in the two groups serve to distinguish transported or reworked specimens from untransported organisms. The amount of fragmentation, abrasion, and disarticulation is a realistic indicator of transport: that is, the least transport, the least fragmentation, while with increasing transport, shells appear increasingly broken or disarticulated. The same observation applies to abrasion and disarticulation. Also, population ratios of adults to juveniles suggest rates of transport. For example, an adult-dominated population suggests increasingly transported specimens. However, one must be cautious in using this parameter because it may also indicate conditions of burial (Palacios-Fest et al. 2001). Carapace/valve ratios are also used to help establish whether the assemblages have or have not been transported.

Sediment Particle Size Analysis

Laboratory Consultants of Tempe, Arizona, performed mechanical particle size analysis of a select group of modern canal and other fluvial samples. Sediment samples that ranged in size from 0.25 to 1.0 cup were first sieved to determine the percentage of gravel (>2.0 mm) present. Then a hydrometer method was used to determine the percentage of sand (.05–2.0 mm), silt (.002–.05 mm), and clay (<.002 mm) present in the remaining nongravel sediment.

Plants Associated with Geological Units

Field observations ascertained the modern plant associations on lands adjacent to canals and other fluvial locations sampled for this study (Table 7). The majority of the plants were established perennials, especially shrubs and small trees. Few plants (*Chenopodium berlandieri, Heliotropium curassavicum,* and *Pluchea sericea*) had flower buds during the winter observation period, and the only fully flowering types (*Hoffmanseggia glauca* and *Lycium fremontii*) were unlikely to contribute much pollen to canal sediments because of their entomophilous (insect-pollinated) nature. Some plants still had fruit clinging from a previous reproductive season, a circumstance of potential value to humans during a relatively dormant time of year for plants.

Sediment Particle Size

The particle size analysis revealed notable variability among the samples analyzed (Table 8). Samples ranged from sand to a clay loam. Gravel generally constituted a small proportion of most samples. The particle size data will be discussed in more detail below.

Pollen

Limitations of Pollen Data and Research Questions

The Latin root of the word "palynology" is *palynos,* meaning dust, and palynology is literally the study of dust, as the size of pollen grains ranges from less than 0.008 mm to 0.1 mm. And like dust, pollen is always in the air; however, the amount and composition vary by season, vegetation, and local climate. Most plant species disperse pollen by one of two methods: wind-pollinated or insect-pollinated. In general, wind-pollinated plants such as pine, sagebrush, and grass produce abundant pollen designed to travel, while insect-pollinated plants, such as cactus and many of the herbs, produce small amounts of pollen designed to hitchhike short distances on insects. For example, one male pinecone may produce more than half a million pollen grains (more than a billion grains from just one tree), whereas some species of plantain (*Plantago*) produce as few as 30 pollen grains per anther (Faegri and Iversen 1989:12). Wind-pollinated plants are typically overrepresented in pollen assemblages, and insect-pollinated plants are usually underrepresented or missed altogether. However, the creative variety of plant reproductive systems leads to many exceptions to these generalizations (Faegri and van der Pijl 1979).

Table 7. Plants Observed at Collecting Stations

Location	Landform	Taxon	Seasonality Data
Northside Canal (CS4)	Canal within T-2 terrace	*Acacia greggii*	C, NF, MF
		Atriplex canescens	C, NF, MF
		Cercidium floridum	C, NF, MF
		Echinochloa colonum	C, NF, MF
		Hoffmannseggia glauca	D, FF, IF/MF
		Larrea sp.	S, NF, NF
		Leptochloa uninervia	C, NF, IF/MF
		Lycium sp.	C, NF, NF
		Parkinsonia sp.	C, NF, NF
		Prosopis sp.	C, NF, NF
		Salsola sp.	C, NF, NF
		Sphaeralcea sp.	C, NF, NF
		Suaeda torreyana	C, NF, MF
		Zizyphus sp.	C, NF, NF
Pima Lateral Canal (CS5)	Canal within T-2 terrace	*Chenopodium berlandieri*	C, FB, NF
		Echinochloa colonum	C, NF, MF
		Heliotropium curassavicum	C, FB, NF
		Leptochloa univervia	D, NF, IF/MF
		Portulaca oleracea	C, NF, MF
		Tamarix sp.	S, NF, NF
Mish Ki Canal (CS6)	Canal within T-2 terrace	*Echinochloa colonum*	C, NF, MF
		Heliotropium curassavicum	S, FB, NF
		Leptochloa uninervia	D, NF, IF/MF
		Prosopis sp.	D, NF, NF
		Salsola sp.	S, NF, NF
		Suaeda torreyana	C, NF, MF
Canal clean out (CS11)		*Distichlis spicata*	D, NF, MF
Holocene fan (CS12)	Ephemeral drainage	*Acacia* aff *greggii*	C, NF, MF
		Cercidium floridum	D, NF, MF
		Cercidium microphyllum	S, NF, MF
		Hymenoclea aff *salsola*	CD, NF, NF
		Larrea sp.	C, NF, NF
		Lycium sp.	C, NF, NF
		Olneya tesota	C, NF, NF
Gila River floodplain (CS19)	Holocene alluvium	*Atriplex lentiformis*	C, NF, MF
		Cercidium sp.	C, NF, NF
		Cruciferae	C, NF, NF
		Dicoria canescens	C, NF, NF
		Hymenoclea aff *salsola*	R, NF, NF
		Isocoma acradenia	R, NF, MF
		Larrea sp.	C, NF, NF
		Pluchea sericea	R, FB, NF
		Prosopis sp.	C, NF, NF
		Salix sp.	C, NF, NF
		Salsola sp.	C, NF, NF
		Tamarix sp.	C, NF, NF
McClellan Wash (CS28)	Holocene alluvium	*Atriplex lentiformis*	C, NF, NF
		Atriplex polycarpa	C, NF, NF
		Poaceae	D, NF, NF
		Isocoma acradenia	R, NF, NF
		Lycium fremontii	C, FB/FF, NF
		Phalaris minor	C, NF, NF
		Pluchea sericea	R, NF, NF
		Prosopis sp.	S, NF, NF
		Salsola sp.	C, NF, NF
		Suaeda torreyana	S, NF, NF
		Tamarix sp.	C, NF, NF
Little Gila River (CS33)	Holocene alluvium	*Atriplex canescens*	C, NF, MF
		Atriplex lentiformis	C, NF, MF
		Casuarina sp.	C, NF, NF
		Asteraceae	C, NF, NF
		Poaceae	C, NF, NF
		Lycium sp.	C, NF, NF
		Nicotiana glauca	S, NF, NF
		Prosopis sp.	C, NF, NF
		Tamarix sp.	D, NF, NF
		Xanthium sp.	S, NF, MF

Abbreviations: aff = affinity with; sp. = species; CS = collecting station; CD = co-dominant; D = dominant; C = common; S = sparse; R = rare; FB = flowers in bud; FF = full flowering; FW = flowers wilted; NF = flower not present; IF = immature fruit; MF = mature fruit; NF = no fruit. Under "Seasonality Data" flower observations are listed before fruit observations.

Table 8. Results of Mechanical Particle Size Analysis of Sediment Samples

Sample Number	Original Vol. (cups)	% Gravel (>2.0mm)	% Sand (0.05–2.0 mm)	% Silt (0.002–0.05 mm)	% Clay (<0.002mm)	Classification
CS4-9	0.5	0.4	6.4	68.0	25.6	Clay loam
CS4-10	0.9	0.2	43.2	23.8	33.0	Clay loam
CS4-11	1.0	1.9	33.3	32.8	34.0	Clay loam
CS4-12	1.0	0.3	24.0	42.0	34.0	Clay loam
CS4-13	1.0	0.2	15.2	44.8	40.0	Silty clay
CS5-14	0.5	1.2	93.4	3.0	3.6	Sand
CS5-15	1.0	13.8	93.4	3.0	3.6	Sand
CS5-16	1.0	1.3	22.0	53.0	25.0	Silty loam
CS6-17	1.0	0.0	91.4	5.0	3.6	Sand
CS6-18	0.5	0.1	29.2	51.8	19.0	Silty loam
CS6-19	0.75	0.1	80.4	10.0	9.6	Loamy sand
CS11-25	0.5	0.6	34.4	48.0	17.6	Loam
CS11-26	0.9	0.7	30.4	42.0	27.6	Clay loam
CS12-27	0.25	4.9	92.4	6.0	1.6	Sand
CS12-28	0.25	17.9	70.4	22.0	7.6	Sandy loam
CS28-60	0.5	0.2	54.4	32.0	13.6	Sandy loam
CS28-61	0.5	1.4	23.4	47.0	29.6	Clay loam
CS33-70	0.75	0.0	46.4	40.0	13.6	Loam
CS33-71	0.75	0.1	46.4	40.0	13.6	Loam

The most common application of palynology is the study of past environments. Paleoecologic studies are typically conducted on stratigraphic series from lakes and bogs because these are the best environments for pollen preservation (anaerobic and acidic) and pollen accumulation rates are relatively constant (Bradley 1999; Faegri and Iversen 1989; Moore et al. 1991). Sediment samples from terrestrial contexts are more complicated. Terrestrial samples contain pollen derived primarily from atmospheric pollen rain entrained in sediment that is exposed to episodic deposition and erosion events (such as slope wash, eolian processes, and bioturbation), which can affect the abundance and composition of soil pollen assemblages. Flowing water, such as the canal and natural fluvial contexts studied here, are the most complicated pollen depositional environments because a mix of terrestrial and fluvial processes are operating.

The complexity of fluvial systems has discouraged research on how pollen arrives at, and becomes incorporated within, water-deposited sediments. A handful of studies from Europe and Canada have focused on stream pollen input into lakes (Bonny 1978; Crowder and Cuddy 1973; Peck 1973; Pennington 1979; Starling and Crowder 1981), but essentially no research has been conducted on the physics of pollen deposition within canal systems. Pollen studies of stream systems have shown that peaks in atmospheric pollen correspond to specific flowering periods and register in water samples (Bonny 1978; Crowder and Cuddy 1973; Peck 1973; Starling and Crowder 1981). Hydraulic sorting of pollen by shape and size has also been investigated (Brush and Brush 1972; Davis and Brubaker 1973; Fall 1987). Pollen investigations of modern alluvium reveal that pollen grains contained in water-deposited sediments arrive at deposition sites by a variety of vectors, including air, water, insect, and reworking of older sediments (Fall 1987; Hevly et al. 1965; Schoenwetter and Doerschlag 1971; Solomon et al. 1982).

In this study, we collected 20 samples from sediments within the bottoms of modern earthen canals and surfaces of natural fluvial contexts along the middle Gila River to examine the following questions. How distinct are the pollen assemblages from different water depositional environments? Are canal pollen assemblages unique? Do individual canals exhibit identifiable signatures? Is there a relationship between sediment particle size and the abundance of pollen? We also examined the issue of sample variability using a set of duplicate samples from the same contexts. To answer these questions, we organized the pollen types into probable source areas and identified key or indicator pollen types and parameters, and then evaluated the data for any significant patterns.

Pollen Types Identified

A surprising diversity of 55 pollen types and one spore was identified among the 20 samples (Table 9; Appendix Table 1). Each pollen type was identified as precisely as possible. Several pollen types could not be assigned to an individual plant species or even family because grain morphologies have not been studied to develop a workable taxonomy. Cheno-am is a category that subsumes species from two plant families, Chenopodiaceae and Amaranthaceae, including both herbs and shrubs that are ubiquitous in the modern Gila Valley. There is more taxonomic division within the Asteraceae family, which has been split into the hi-spine, long-spine, and low-spine Asteraceae and the Liguliflorae tribe. Even in the four-way Asteraceae split, several plant genera are encompassed in each category (Table 9). Common names are used to discuss the pollen results, except for the Asteraceae and cheno-ams.

Analysts also took note of pollination mode (wind or insect), the pollination or flowering season, and sample frequency for each pollen type (Kearney and Peebles 1960; Rea 1997; Shreve and Wiggins 1964; Turner et al. 1995). The common pollen types identified in this study are wind-pollinated, and some species flower year-round. Many Sonoran Desert plants, such as creosote bush, are opportunistic, flowering any time adequate moisture is present. Several species, such as mesquite, will flower twice a year, once with spring rain and once during the summer monsoonal rains. The generalist flowering strategy often limits interpretations of seasonal signals in Southwestern pollen data, except for a few plants with limited flowering periods, such as cacti, juniper, pine, and oak.

The most abundant pollen types identified in all samples were cheno-am, hi-spine and low-spine Asteraceae, and grass, followed by the conifers (pine, pinyon pine, and juniper). These seven taxa account for 73–92% of the pollen counted in all 20 samples (Figure 5). Several rare pollen types were identified only in one to two samples (Appendix Table 1): *Acalypha*, milkweed, agave, chicory tribe (Liguliflorae), dock, hibiscus, squash, ocotillo, and creosote bush pollen were identified in only one sample each, and grease wood, gray thorn, lily family, and pea family pollen were identified in two samples each. Most of the rare pollen types come from insect-pollinated plants with specific flowering seasons, and although their occurrence is interesting, the research questions are best addressed by patterns in the dominant pollen types.

Cultivated crops were represented in six samples by cotton and corn, and possibly squash. Commercial-scale farms growing a variety of crops, including corn and cotton, line the Gila River valley, and the cultigens identified probably reflect modern farming. However, prehistoric cultigen pollen could also be incorporated, as modern surface samples far from modern farms but close to Hohokam sites often contain cultigen pollen. Both Twin Buttes fan samples (CS12) produced cotton and corn pollen, the highest cultigen frequency from any collecting station. This expression could be pollen from prehistoric farming or could be derived from modern agricultural pollen blowing up onto the fan surface. Most sources state that cotton is strictly insect-pollinated and self-pollinated, but some evidence indicates that cotton pollen is blown about by wind (Ahlstrom and Cummings 1998; Cantley 1991:86–87).

Three pollen taxa are interpreted to represent exotic, introduced plants: pecan, crane's bill, and elm. These three taxa produce taxonomically distinct pollen grains. Pecan is planted in orchards and yards throughout the region. Crane's bill is generally interpreted as an exotic, introduced probably by the Spanish. However, one native species (*Erodium texanum*) may have been more widespread prehistorically. Elm pollen occurring in two samples is attributed to the exotic Siberian elm because no elms (*Ulmus* sp.) are native to Arizona. Two other pollen types—cereal grass and the summer poppy or goat's head type—could represent native or introduced genera, but these taxa more likely reflect the presence of introduced weeds. Most of the exotic plant species in Arizona outcompete native plants, even native weeds and other ephemeral plants. The disturbed soils of the natural fluvial and canal contexts sampled in this study are prime weed habitat.

Pollen Source Areas

Source area categories serve to organize the diverse range of pollen taxa identified into logical groups. The idea of source areas is important because the divisions have implications for whether pollen has arrived at deposition sites by air or water. The pollen types identified in this study were assigned to three categories (Table 9) defined as follows:

Table 9. Pollen Types Identified and Interpreted Source Areas

Pollen Source Area	Taxon	Common Name
EXTRALOCAL TO REGIONAL ATMOSPHERIC POLLEN AND WATERBORNE POLLEN	*Pinus* sp.	Pine
	Pinus sp. (pinyon type)	Pinyon pine
	Juniperus sp.	Juniper
	Quercus sp.	Oak
	Juglans sp.	Walnut
	Rosaceae	Rose family
	Artemisia sp.	Sagebrush
	Celtis sp.	Hackberry
	Dodonaea sp.	Hopbush
	Simmondsia sp.	Jojoba
WATER INDICATORS	*Typha* sp.	Cattail
	Salix sp.	Willow
	Cyperaceae	Sedge
LOCAL TO EXTRALOCAL TREES AND SHRUBS	*Acacia* sp.	Cat claw
	Cercidium sp.	Palo verde
	Fouquieria sp.	Ocotillo
	Larrea sp.	Creosote
	Prosopis sp.	Mesquite
	Ephedra sp.	Mormon tea
	Rhamnaceae	Gray thorn, crucillo
	Sarcobatus sp.	Greasewood
LOCAL TO EXTRALOCAL HERBS AND SHRUBS	Cheno-am	Includes several weed, herb, & shrub *Chenopodium* and *Atriplex* spp. plus tumbleweed, seepweed, & others
	Tidestroemia sp.	Tidestroemia
	Hi-spine Asteraceae	Includes brittlebush, arrow-weed, aster, desert marigold, & others
	Liguliflorae	Chicory tribe: wire lettuce, dandelion, & others
	Long-spine Asteraceae	Cf. sunflower (*Helianthus*) type
	Low-spine Asteraceae	Ragweed/bur sage (*Ambrosia*) & burro brush *(Hymenoclea)*
	Poaceae	Grass family
	Boerhaavia sp.	Spiderling
	Rumex sp.	Cf. dock

Table 9. Pollen Types Identified and Interpreted Source Areas *(continued)*

Pollen Source Area	Taxon	Common Name
LOCAL TO EXTRALOCAL HERBS AND SHRUBS (continued)	*Sphaeralcea* sp.	Globe mallow
	Eriogonum sp.	Buckwheat
	Brassicaceae	Mustard family
	Onagraceae	Evening primrose family
	Euphorbiaceae	Spurge family
	Plantago sp.	Plantain; Indian wheat
	Cf. *Hibiscus* sp. (Malvaceae)	Cf. Hibiscus
	Polemoniaceae	Jacob's ladder family
	Cf. *Acalypha* sp.	Cf. *Acalypha*
	Cf. *Asclepias* sp.	Cf. milkweed
	Fabaceae	Pea family includes several herb & shrub genera
LOCAL TO EXTRALOCAL CACTI, YUCCA, AND AGAVE	*Agave*	Agave
	Liliaceae	Includes yucca, wild onion, & others
	Cactaceae	Includes saguaro, hedgehog, & other cacti
	Cylindropuntia	Cholla
	Platyopuntia	Prickly pear
CULTIGENS	*Cucurbita* sp.	Includes squash & buffalo gourd
	Gossypium sp.	Cotton
	Zea mays sp.	Corn/maize
EXOTIC WEEDS — LOCAL	*Kallstroemia/Tribulus* sp.	Summer poppy/goats head
	Large Poaceae	Cf. cereal grasses
	Erodium sp.	Crane's bill; filaree
	Ulmus cf. *pumila*	Siberian elm
	Carya sp.	Pecan
SPECIAL POLLEN CATEGORIES	Unknown A	Mustard/willow type, possibly creosote bush or tamarisk
	Trilete spore with perine	Trilete spore in sac

Abbreviation: Cf. = compares favorably

36

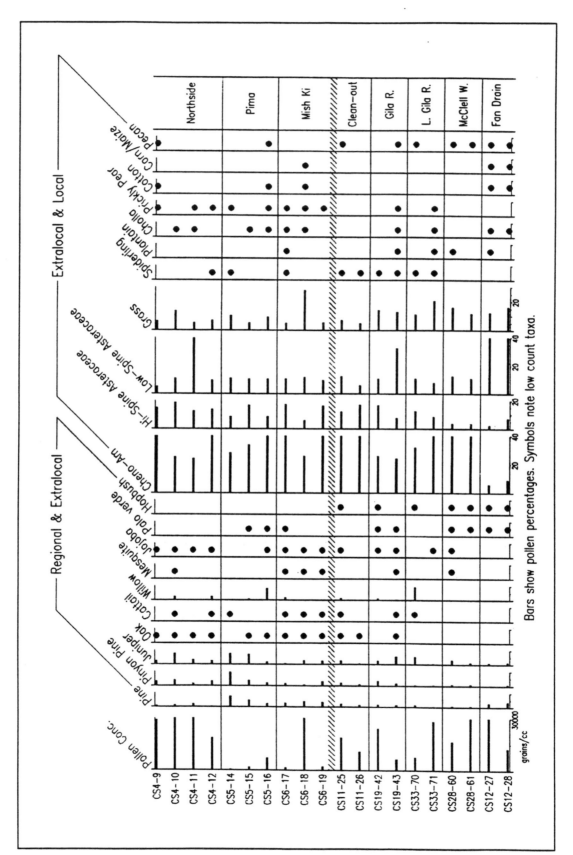

Figure 5. Pollen results from modern canals and fluvial sites, Gila River Indian Community, middle Gila River. Hatched line indicates the main division separating Canals (above hatching) from terrestrial and ephemeral fluvial contexts (below hatching).

a. The local to extralocal category refers to pollen representing vegetation within 1–5 km of the collecting station. For most stations, this source area is the Gila River valley, which includes Sonoran Desert vegetation and the vegetation growing in human-altered environments, such as fields, roadsides, and construction sites. Lower bajada vegetation communities, such as north of the Northside Canal, may also be included. Local to extralocal pollen types are assumed to be deposited mainly from atmospheric pollen rain with a smaller water-deposited component.

b. The extralocal to regional category encompasses the area farther than 5 km away, drawing from the entire Gila River drainage basin, which includes pine forests, pinyon and juniper woodland, and chaparral communities in addition to Sonoran Desert vegetation. The extralocal to regional source areas are represented by pollen from pines and juniper, as well as vegetation such as hackberry and jojoba. A significant component of the extralocal to regional pollen taxa are interpreted to represent water-transported pollen.

c. The main water indicators are cattail and willow. Sedge pollen was identified in low numbers from only one sample (CS33-70). Cattail and willow pollen is probably deposited mainly from flowing water but represents upstream riparian vegetation lining rivers and canals.

Pollen Signatures

Pollen results for dominant taxa and some of the key pollen types (documented in Appendix Table 1) are graphically displayed in Figure 5. The graphs in Figure 5 emphasize the abundance of the dominant pollen types (cheno-am, Asteraceae, and grass). Analysts referred to these graphs and source area information in Table 9 to select a set of pollen types to test whether canal pollen assemblages can be discriminated from those derived from natural fluvial and terrestrial contexts.

A cluster analysis was performed on select pollen data using CONISS, a computer statistical program developed by Grim (1987) specifically for analyzing pollen data within *Tilia,* a software package written by Grim for graphing pollen data. The several analyses run on the samples used different combinations of pollen types to explore which taxa were the most sensitive for discriminating canals. For each run, the pollen data were entered as raw counts and converted to proportions, which ensures that the set of variables for each sample is normalized to 1. Clusters were defined on unconstrained samples by square root transformation and incremental sum of squares (Grim 1987). The best analysis was run with nine pollen types on 18 samples (Figure 6). The two canal clean-out samples (CS11) were excluded because they produced mixed water and terrestrial signals, which makes sense for the context but added unnecessary noise to the analysis.

38

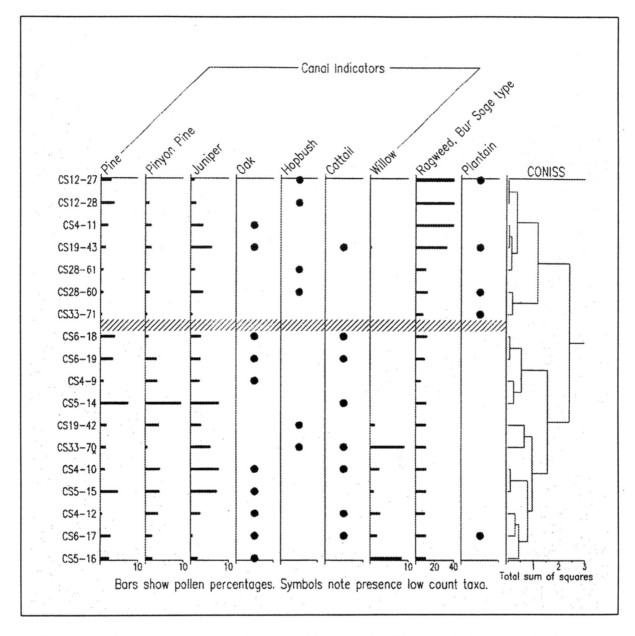

Figure 6. Cluster analysis of pollen results. Hatched line indicates main division separating canals (below hatching) from terrestrial and ephemeral fluvial contexts (above hatching).

The cluster analysis generally separated canals from natural fluvial contexts, except for two floodplain samples (CS19-42 and CS33-70) that clustered with canals and one canal sample (CS4-11) that was paired with a Gila River floodplain sample (CS19-43). The cluster analysis shows that the best indicators of canals were the regional trees (pine, pinyon pine, juniper, and oak) and water types (cattail and willow). Pollen percentages of regional trees were maximal in the largest canal (Pima Lateral Canal [CS5]) and decreased to the smaller canals (CS4 and CS6) and the Gila River (CS19) and Little Gila River (CS33) floodplains (Figures 5 and 6).

No definitive pollen types separated fluvial or alluvial contexts from canals, although the strongest pattern in the cluster analysis was the separation of the Holocene fan samples (CS12) by high values of low-spine Asteraceae (Figure 5). The low-spine Asteraceae pollen in the CS12 samples undoubtedly represents burro brush, a dominant shrub around the collecting station. Plantain and hopbush were associated with the natural fluvial and terrestrial collecting stations; however, the numerical influence of these two low-count types was minimal. The most abundant pollen types have the strongest effect on the calculations, and the analysis could be fine-tuned by weighting other key, but less abundant, taxa.

Other less abundant types that can be subjectively interpreted as key indicators include several of the extralocal to local taxa. Canals were characterized by a higher representation of mesquite, jojoba, and prickly pear pollen (Figure 5). The natural fluvial sites (Gila River [CS19] and Little Gila River [CS33] floodplains) were characterized by more juniper, cattail, willow, jojoba, and spiderling pollen than the ephemeral McClellan Wash (CS28) and Twin Buttes fan (CS12). McClellan Wash and Twin Buttes fan samples were distinguished by plantain, pecan, and hopbush pollen.

Individual canal signatures can also be interpreted. Two canal samples (CS5-16 and CS6-18), composed of dark sediment considered highly organic in content, were termed "black muck" samples. Pollen results from the two black muck samples were discounted in describing individual canal signatures: both samples (especially CS6-18) produced assemblages that contrasted with other samples in the same canal. One interesting note is that cultigen pollen was documented from both black muck samples yet was rare from all other contexts. Only one other canal sample (CS4-9) produced crop pollen (cotton). The canal clean-out samples (CS11) were also discounted in interpreting these data. The results from CS11 were a mix of terrestrial and water-transported signals, characterized by high percentages of the dominant pollen types (cheno-am, Asteraceae, and grass) and the presence of water indicators (cattail and willow), as well as jojoba, hopbush, and spiderling pollen.

Samples from the Pima Lateral Canal (CS5), the largest canal sampled, produced the lowest pollen concentration values of any collecting station and the most regional pollen signal with high percentages of conifers and low to no representation of the extralocal taxa. Pollen concentration was maximum in the Northside Canal (CS4) samples and regional conifer pollen was high, but extralocal taxa (especially jojoba and prickly pear) were also represented. The smallest canal, the Mish Ki Canal (CS6), was characterized by low pollen concentration, low pinyon pine and juniper percentages, and high representation of cattail, mesquite, jojoba, and prickly pear. The Mish Ki Canal samples produced the most mixed assemblages of all 10 canal samples.

Complacent pollen types were also interpreted from the results. Complacent taxa are defined as those that are not unique to specific samples or contexts or do not produce a consistent pattern of abundance between contexts. Cheno-am, sunflower family, and grass pollen were abundant in all samples. Likewise, crane's bill and buckwheat pollen occurred in all contexts, suggesting these are not useful context indicator species, at least in this set of samples.

Pollen Assemblages and Correspondence to Modern Vegetation

It is difficult to assess how well the pollen assemblages represent local vegetation, partly because pollen taxa are generally not identifiable to species. For example, several shrub and herb species documented growing at each collecting station produce pollen that would be recorded in the broad cheno-am category. Another confounding factor is the insect-pollination of many common desert plants such as palo verde, creosote bush, mesquite, cat claw, and gray thorn, which makes them less likely to be recovered from sediment samples than wind-pollinated taxa.

The best pollen correspondence between pollen and modern vegetation is from the Twin Buttes alluvial fan (CS12). Palo verde and burro brush are the two dominant plants on the fan (Table 7), and both pollen samples produced palo verde pollen and the maximum low-spine Asteraceae (subsumes burro brush) percentages out of all the samples (Figure 5). The worst correspondence between pollen and modern vegetation is in the canal samples, as shown by a higher representation of regional to extralocal taxa (Figures 5 and 6). Plantain (*Plantago*) pollen, considered to be a sensitive record of local plants, was associated with the floodplain samples (CS19 and CS33) and Twin Buttes fan samples (CS12) but was almost entirely absent from the canal samples. Field personnel did not note the presence of plantain during the winter plant surveys, but this small annual is normally invisible until triggered by spring rains. Crane's bill is another early spring plant that was probably missed during winter surveys but may also be a sensitive local pollen indicator.

Pollen Variability

We collected duplicate samples at all of the collecting stations to investigate the question of sample variability. Variability is an inherent attribute of pollen data, reflecting the dynamic interaction between pollen production, dispersal, and environment. The clearest expression of variability in this study is in pollen concentration values. The maximum concentration out of all 20 samples is from the Mish Ki Canal black muck sample (CS6-18) at 162,419 gr/cc (grains per cubic centimeter). The minimum concentration value is from a Pima Lateral Canal sample (CS5-14) at 362 gr/cc.

If the Mish Ki Canal black muck sample is excluded, concentration values between duplicate samples vary by 1.5 to 4.0 times higher in one sample over another. Some samples, such as the two Mish Ki Canal fill samples (CS6-17 and CS6-19), exhibit essentially identical assemblages in terms of pollen abundance and percentages. Taxon richness (diversity) varies between replicate samples by one to seven types, and the relative percentages of individual pollen types vary from less than 1% to greater than 30%. Canal samples are characterized by significant spikes in both concentration and percentage values, but floodplain and ephemeral wash samples produced less variable concentrations.

These results emphasize that variability can be a significant factor in pollen data. Few studies have addressed pollen sample variability, and palynologists have developed no guidelines for how many samples are adequate to control for variability. Interpretations of trends or patterns should not be based on single or even a few pollen samples. Series of samples from comparable contexts and multiple samples from individual contexts will yield more significant patterns and trends than single samples.

Sediment Particle Size, Pollen Abundance, and Hydrologic Interpretations from Canal Samples

If the modern canal pollen assemblages are primarily water-deposited, pollen abundance should correlate with sediment texture because pollen travels and deposits in flowing water by the same physical laws that govern the hydraulic behavior of other particles (Brush and Brush 1972; Fall 1987). Investigations of prehistoric Hohokam canals in the Phoenix Basin (Smith 1995, 1997a, 1997b, 1997c) have shown that pollen abundance, as measured by concentration, is higher in fine-grained sediments (such as silt and clay) than in coarse-grained sediments (such as sand). Samples from Hohokam canals with greater than 30% sand typically produce low pollen concentrations of less than 4,000 gr/cc (Figure 7).

Pollen concentrations in the 10 Gila River canal samples from the modern analog study have been compared to those of 59 prehistoric canal samples derived from Salt River canals (Figure 7). The Gila River canal samples are mostly sand, with greater than 30% sand in six samples and three samples containing 22–29% sand (Table 8). The Gila River canal samples fit the overall trend for decreasing pollen concentration with increasing sand content, although the majority of the modern canal samples plot at the upper range of concentrations above prehistoric canal samples. This result may reflect better pollen preservation, which would be expected in modern samples compared to the prehistoric samples, which date primarily to the Hohokam Classic period.

The black muck sample (CS6-18) from the Mish Ki Canal, with greater than 29% sand, had the maximum pollen concentration in any sample. This anomalous sample apparently contains a pollen-rich organic component. Organic materials in sediment samples are generally not accounted for in sediment particle size analyses, but they could be, as a reasonable predictor of pollen presence.

The correspondence between particle size and pollen abundance is interpreted to relate to the hydrologic environment during which sediments were deposited. High-energy, turbulent flows carry coarser particles; and when water velocity decreases, sand is deposited. Lower-energy flows transport silt and clay that is deposited as flow decreases. The minimal pollen concentrations in the Pima Lateral and Mish Ki canals are consistent with fast, turbulent flows (indicated by the sandy sediments), and the moderate concentration values in the Northside Canal match the interpretation of slow, low-energy flows (indicated by the silt and clay texture).

42

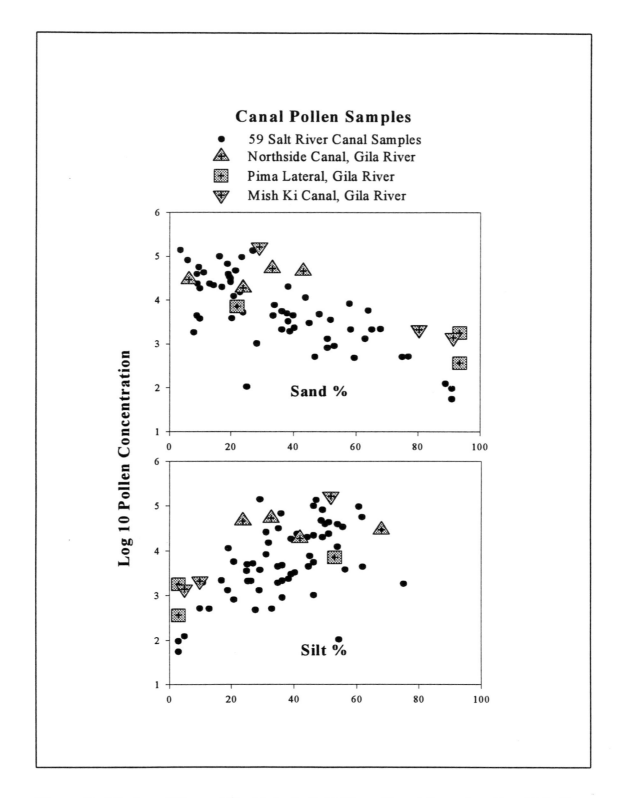

Figure 7. Modern Gila and Prehistoric Salt River Canal Samples. Log10 Pollen Concentration Graphed Against Sediment Particle Size Data

Molluscs and Ostracodes

In general, the molluscs and ostracodes were contained within canal and other fluvial sediments that consisted of clay loam to sandy loam. Mollusc and ostracode content (total and relative abundance), taphonomic features, and other materials present in the canals are summarized in Appendix Tables 2 and 3. A characteristic common to both molluscs and ostracodes is the lack of soft parts and original coloring when recently dead, making it harder to identify them based on remaining shell traits.

Ostracode valves are usually clear but retain for some time the colors of the food, showing the species pattern, as well as chitinous material. The mollusc species recovered for this study are usually whitish opaque, but modern specimens would include the soft body and radula if alive at the time of sampling. Evidence suggests that most of the organisms were washed into the collection sites and then developed local populations. The micropaleontology of molluscs and ostracodes are discussed separately below.

The freshwater mussel *Anodonta californiensis*, frequently recovered in archaeological sites in the Sonoran Desert, was missing from the canal samples. Apparently historical factors, such as the disappearance of surface waters, the damming of rivers, and the loss of certain host fish, have led to its decline in the twentieth century (Bequaert and Miller 1973:220–223). However, investigators may reasonably expect to find evidence of this edible mussel in prehistoric middens associated with archaeological sites along the Gila River, as well as in prehistoric canal sediments, as these mussels have been reported from Snaketown (Bequaert and Miller 1973:222).

Mollusc Signatures

Molluscs were recovered from all 17 sediment samples reported here, although 4 samples had very small, unidentifiable shell fragments (Appendix Table 2). Two additional Holocene fan ephemeral wash samples (CS12) lacking mollusc remains have been eliminated from consideration. Low mollusc diversity and abundance characterize the area. Of the six recovered species, five are gastropods: *Helisoma tenue* (planorbid), *Physa virgata* (pulmonate), *Succinea* sp. cf. *S. luteola sonorensis* (terrestrial pulmonate), *Laevapex* (*Ferrisia*) *californica* (Ancylidae), and *Stagnicola elodes* (Lymnaeidae). One pelecypod species, *Sphaerium transversum* (Sphaeriidae), was also recovered.

Bequaert and Miller (1973) and Miksicek (1985) say that the genus *Stagnicola* was a widespread group in the past in Arizona. *Stagnicola elodes,* documented here, was reported by Bequaert and Miller (1973) for northern Arizona only. Miksicek (1985) and Vokes and Miksicek (1987) do not report this species, but *S. bulimoides* differs from *S. elodes* in having a more elongated aperture. The identification of *S. elodes* in this study is based on Webb (1942), but no reference material was available to credit or discredit it. *Laevapex* (*Ferrisia*) *californica* is not commonly reported from Arizona (Bequaert and Miller, 1973). This is the

44

first identification of this species in irrigation canals. However, Bequaert and Miller (1973) suggest that this freshwater limpet is probably more common in the state than has been reported previously.

Population size was low, ranging from 2 to 51 individuals in any given sample, with *P. virgata* (*N*=37) and *S. transversum* (*N*=36) the most common, followed by *Succinea* sp. (*N*=14) and *H. tenue* (*N*=10). The relative abundance of mollusc species varied by collecting station. *Helisoma tenue* (4%–25%) and *P. virgata* (4%–100%) occurred in most collecting stations (eight and ten samples, respectively), followed by *Succinea* sp. cf. *S. luteola* (8%–19%, present in six samples). *Laevapex (Ferrisia) californica* (8%) and *Stagnicola elodes* (2%) each occurred only once in the record. *Sphaerium transversum* (pelecypod) was an important element where present (4%–63%).

To determine autochthony of the assemblage, analysts measured taphonomic features. Fragmentation rates are high across the area, ranging from 20% to 100%, suggesting transported assemblages. Occasionally, some fragments or specimens show evidence of encrustation, coating, or abrasion (5–15%). Where complete specimens were recovered the adult/juvenile (a/j) ratio was used. Three samples (CS6-19, CS28-61, and CS33-70) contained only adult populations, again suggestive of transported assemblages. All other samples generally contained more juveniles than adults (ratio: 0.08–0.75). In the case of pelecypods, the articulation ratio was also considered. Of the five samples where clams were reported, articulated valves occurred only in one (CS6-18).

Based upon the ecological requirements of the mollusc species present and their streamflow implications (Table 10), four assemblages were identified. Assemblage 1, dominated by a species *(P. virgata)* adapted to a wide range of ecological conditions (Vokes and Miksicek 1987), indicates a slow streamflow. The co-occurrence of this species with ostracodes also suggests low-energy conditions. Assemblage 2, dominated by a terrestrial species (*Succinea* sp. cf. *S. luteola sonorensis*), reflects moist, well-vegetated habitats

Table 10. Ecological Requirements of Mollusc Species Recovered from GRIC Lands

Species	Habitat	Permanence
Helisoma tenue	Streams, ponds, lakes, canals	Permanent or ephemeral or moist soil
Physa virgata	Streams, lakes, ponds, canals	Permanent or ephemeral
Stagnicola elodes	Ponds, lakes, marshes	Permanent or ephemeral
Succinea sp. cf. *S. luteola sonorensis*	Riparian, marshes	Moist soils
Laevapex (Ferrisia) californica	Springs, lakes, streams	Permanent
Sphaerium transversum	Streams, canals, lakes	Permanent

Note: all species are eurythermic in temperature.
Sources: Bequaert and Miller 1973; Miksicek 1989; Vokes and Miksicek 1987; Webb 1942

adjacent to marshes and watercourses (Vokes and Miksicek 1987). The co-occurrence of a terrestrial mollusc associated with ostracodes implies riparian conditions. Assemblage 3, dominated by a species capable of living in both muddy and sandy substrates (*Sphaerium transversum*), indicates moderately low energy conditions (Vokes and Miksicek 1987). The co-occurrence of this species with *Stagnicola elodes* and ostracodes supports a slow streamflow environment. Assemblage 4, characterized by the high fragmentation of *H. tenue* (only species present), suggests fast flow conditions (Miksicek 1989).

Ostracode Signatures

Fourteen analyzed sediment samples contained ostracodes, reported for total and relative abundance (Appendix Table 3). Additional samples from an ephemeral wash (CS12) and the Little Gila River floodplain (CS33) were devoid of specimens. In total, nine ostracode species were recognized: *Limnocythere staplini, Ilyocypris bradyi, Cypridopsis vidua, Heterocypris glaucus, Candona caudata, Candona patzcuaro, Herpetocypris brevicaudata, Cypria ophthalmica*, and an unidentified species. *Ilyocypris bradyi* (N=216, identified in 12 samples) was the most common and abundant species present, followed by *C. vidua* (N=72, 9 samples), *H. brevicaudata* (N=71, 10 samples), and *L. staplini* (N=75, 6 samples). Other species occurred occasionally throughout the area. All collecting stations were characterized by low to moderately low populations (2–140 specimens) and low diversity (1–6 species). Small sample size appears to be the result of stressing conditions when canals were active.

Low abrasion and fragmentation were recorded (5–15%), with the exception of sample CS6-17 (60%). Other taphonomic features (encrustation, coating, redox index, and color) showed minimal, if any, alteration. The taphonomic properties of each sample were used to establish the origin of the specimens—that is, allochthonous (formed elsewhere) versus autochthonous (formed in place)—and the significance of the data (Delorme 1969, 1989; Forester 1988; Palacios-Fest 1997a, 1997c). Generally, the assemblages appear autochthonous in origin.

Based on the ecological requirements of ostracode species present (Table 11), at least four assemblages are well defined in terms of their temperature, salinity, and other water chemistry tolerances. Assemblage I is dominated by *I. bradyi*, alternating with *L. staplini, H. brevicaudata, C. vidua*, and *C. patzcuaro* (minor presence of *C. ophthalmica, H. glaucus*, and *C. caudata* also contributes to this group). Assemblage II is dominated by *L. staplini* with strong presence of *I. bradyi, H. brevicaudata*, and *C. vidua* but poor occurrence of *C. patzcuaro* and *H. glaucus*. Assemblage III consists of *C. vidua* accompanied by *I. bradyi, H. brevicaudata*, and *H. glaucus*. Assemblage IV is monospecific or composed of two species with one feature in common, that is, they grow under fast streamflow conditions. The faunal associations recognized in this investigation characterized a streamflow system evolving from freshwater to the type II water pathway (Ca^{2+}-enriched associated with Na^+, Mg^{2+}, and SO_4^{2-}) of Eugster and Hardie (1978). Basically, river (fresh) water entered the canals and

46

slowly evaporated. As it did, the water chemistry changed from freshwater to saline, and because the water was saturated in calcium, it became enriched in this ion. Assemblages I and III represent the time of water input into the canals. The transition from Assemblages I and III to Assemblage II is consistent with gradual salinization of canal waters, at a time of slow or no water input into the canals. In contrast, Assemblage IV reflects episodes of fast streamflow and reworking of organisms into the collecting station sampled.

Table 11. Ecological Requirements of Ostracode Species Recovered from GRIC Lands

Species	Habitat	Salinity	References
Ilyocypris bradyi	Streams, ponds	100 - 4,000 ppm	Palacios-Fest 1994
Herpetocypris brevicaudata	Springs, streams	200 - 3,000 ppm	Forester 1991
Heterocypris glaucus	Springs, seeps, streams	750 - 4,000 ppm	Delorme 1970
Cypridopsis vidua	Springs, streams, lakes	100 - 4,000 ppm	Palacios-Fest 1994
Candona patzcuaro	Lakes, ponds, canals	200 - 5,000 ppm	Palacios-Fest 1994
Candona caudata	Lakes, ponds, canals	100 - 4,000 ppm	Eyles and Schwarcz 1991
Cypria ophthalmica	Lakes, ponds	100 - 4,000 ppm	Delorme 1970
Limnocythere staplini	Lakes, ponds, canals	500 - 75,000 ppm	Palacios-Fest 1994

Note: all species are eurythermic in temperature and have freshwater to Ca-rich water chemistry requirement; all require permanent water source, with the exception of *Limnocythere staplini*, which requires permanent or ephemeral water source.

Correspondence between Mollusc and Ostracode Assemblages

The faunal associations and relationships among organisms, sediments, and taphonomic features are summarized in Table 12. The assemblage numbers do not necessarily correspond with each other; instead, they reflect the specific conditions for the given group and were correlated with the environmental requirements observed in each sample to establish a coherent reconstruction.

Table 12. Faunal Associations and Correlation between Micro-invertebrate Groups and Sedimentologic Characteristics of Modern GRIC Samples

Collecting Station-Sample	Assemblage		Mollusc Taphonomy	Particle Size	Interpre-tation	Location	Remarks
	Molluscs	Ostracodes					
CS4-9	2	I	Strongly fragmented	Clay loam (68% silt; 26% clay)	Slow/marsh	Northside Canal	
CS4-10	1	I	Strongly fragmented	Clay loam (43% sand; 33% clay)	Moderately slow/stream	"	
CS4-11		I	Strongly fragmented	Clay loam (34% clay; 33% sand)	Slow/stream	"	Reworked molluscs
CS4-12	1	II	Moderately fragmented	Clay loam (42% silt; 34% clay)	Slow/pond	"	
CS4-13	1	I	Weakly fragmented	Silty clay (45% silt; 40% clay)	Slow/pond	"	
CS5-14	3	I	Weakly fragmented	Sand (93%)	Moderately fast/stream	Pima Lateral Canal	
CS5-15	3	I	Weakly fragmented	Sand (93%)	Moderately fast/stream or riparian	"	
CS5-16		I	Strongly fragmented	Silty loam (53% silt)	Moderately slow/stream	"	Reworked molluscs
CS6-17	1	III	Moderately fragmented	Sand (91%)	Moderately slow/stream	Mish Ki Road Canal	
CS6-18	3	I	Moderately fragmented	Silty loam (52% silt; 29% sand)	Moderately slow/stream	"	
CS6-19	3	IV	Moderately fragmented	Loamy sand (80% sand)	Moderate stream	"	
CS11-25	2	I	Strongly fragmented	Loam (48% silt; 34% sand)	Moderately slow/stream or riparian	Canal clean-out	
CS11-26	4	III	Strongly fragmented	Clay loam (42% silt; 30% sand)	Slow or still/pond	"	
CS28-61	4	IV	Strongly fragmented	Clay loam (47% silt; 30% clay)	Moderately fast/stream	McClellan Wash	
CS33-70	4		Strongly fragmented	Loam (46% sand; 40% silt)	Moderately fast/stream	Little Gila River	

<u>Note</u>: to minimize the potential for confusion, ostracode assemblages are given in Roman numerals, while mollusc assemblages are given in Arabic numerals.

The co-occurrence of the ostracodes *I. bradyi*, *L. staplini*, and *C. vidua* with the molluscs *H. tenue* and *P. virgata* is consistent with the typical water chemistry of the area, dilute Ca^{2+}-rich (type II of Eugster and Hardie, 1978). *Ilyocypris bradyi*, a streamflow species, is strongly associated with abundant fragments of unidentified molluscs observed in most collecting stations. The occurrence of a homogenous population of *P. virgata* with a diverse ostracode assemblage in the Northside Canal collecting station (CS4-13) indicates stable conditions at this site, such as dilute Ca^{2+}-rich, permanent (long-term), slow-flowing water. In general, the faunal assemblages and lithology suggest that the following collecting stations represent low to moderately low energy conditions: Northside Canal (CS4), McClellan Wash (CS28), and the Little Gila River (CS33). In contrast, the monospecific ostracode assemblage of *I. bradyi* at the Pima Lateral Canal collecting station (CS5-14) associated with a diverse mollusc assemblage dominated by the pelecypod *Sphaerium transversum* indicates the relatively high energy conditions required by this clam. Hence, the samples from the Pima Lateral Canal (CS5) mainly reflect moderately high energy conditions. The dominance of one group or the other does not necessarily imply changing conditions but a microenvironmental response to the space and resources available.

Some collecting stations show mixed conditions from slow to fast streamflow conditions, for example, the Mish Ki Canal (CS6) and canal clean-out samples (CS11). Two Mish Ki Canal samples (CS6-17 and CS6-18) are both dominated by the gastropod *P. virgata* strongly associated with the ostracode *H. brevicaudata*. The pelecypod *S. transversum* and the ostracode *I. bradyi* (requiring continuous streamflow) are still present. *S. transversum* consists of disarticulated valves in a clayey silt deposit that may not represent the species autoecology. One of the samples (CS6-18) also contains *Stagnicola elodes*, a paludal species uncommon in southern Arizona (Bequaert and Miller 1973).

Mollusc and Ostracode Variability

Faunal assemblages in the analyzed settings reflect a variety of conditions. These include stable energy characteristics (Pima Lateral Canal and Northside Canal), where either high energy or low energy dominates, and mixed-energy conditions (Mish Ki Canal). The Northside Canal is characterized by low energy associated with high diversity and abundance of ostracodes and molluscs. All nine ostracode species occur in one or another sample. The most diverse samples at CS4 (Northside Canal) are 10, 11, 12, and 13, with sample 12 holding the richest population of ostracodes (Appendix Table 3). Molluscs, in contrast, are not as diverse in this location, where only three species are represented by 1–5 specimens (Appendix Table 2). The relatively high abundance of *I. bradyi* in all samples from the Northside Canal is consistent with the streamflow interpretation from the sedimentology and ostracode sections of this report. The taphonomic features recorded in this canal suggest that ostracode populations thrived locally as a result of low-energy flow.

In contrast, the largest of the canals, Pima Lateral Canal (CS5), is a high-energy environment where the faunal assemblages are less diverse and abundant than in the low-energy environment just discussed. *I. bradyi* is still the dominant ostracode confirming the origin of the specimens (fluvial transport). Molluscs (for example, the clam *Sphaerium transversum*) are significantly more diverse and abundant in this canal than in the Northside Canal, demonstrating their dependence on well-aerated conditions.

The mixed-energy environments or those with strong evidence of clean-out activity show the lowest diversity and abundance of specimens, probably as a result of unstable conditions in the case of the Mish Ki Canal (CS6) or destruction by the clean-out (CS11) activity. Occurrence of molluscs is more consistent than that of ostracodes that are limited to a few specimens of, mainly, *I. bradyi*. The presence of *S. transversum* and *P. virgata* indicates the mixing nature of the environment, the latter common in low-energy conditions. It is relevant to note that clean-out samples show a mix of assemblages similar to Mish Ki Canal samples; therefore, clean-out sediments must be recognized in the field to avoid a misinterpretation.

A comparison of the three canals with natural streams or channels (McClellan Wash [CS28] and the Little Gila River [CS33]) demonstrates that the organisms were transported by flowing waters. Extremely low ostracode abundance and diversity are recorded in these non-canal sites. Mostly fragmented mollusc shells confirm this interpretation.

Sediment Particle Size and Micro-invertebrate Assemblages

Analysts identified a correlation between faunal assemblages and type of sediment (Table 12). The Northside Canal (CS4), characterized by a clay loam and a diverse and abundant faunal composition, suggests low-energy conditions that prevailed long enough to allow settlement of numerous species (see Appendix Tables 2 and 3). Similarly, the Pima Lateral Canal (CS5), reflecting high-energy conditions, is marked by coarser sediments than the Northside Canal and is associated with a less diverse and abundant fauna, dominated by some species that require well-aerated conditions. In contrast, the Mish Ki Canal reveals mixed-energy conditions characterized by both the sediments and the faunal assemblages. Interpretation of environments such as the Mish Ki Canal are puzzling because the signals are contradictory. One must be cautious and collect as many field data as possible when studying canals.

Clean-out sediments from canals are not recommended for analysis of micro-invertebrates, as the signals are confusing but also irrelevant, because most shells have been destroyed and will not reflect living or depositional conditions. For example, the sediment composition at CS11 suggests either fast or slow flow, but faunal elements are highly fragmented and scarce. It does not appear that molluscs and ostracodes in clean-out sediments will help with environmental reconstructions.

A direct cause-and-effect link between canal processes and biological assemblages has been assumed in previous studies of prehistoric canals. In this study, we have investigated this assumption with samples from modern canal systems and natural fluvial sites. The results from the pollen and micro-invertebrate data answer the study's main research goal: canals can be discriminated from river floodplains and ephemeral flowing water contexts by their biological assemblages. A corollary of this conclusion is that biological assemblages in sediments from natural aquatic and fluvial systems (lakes and rivers) or terrestrial contexts (bajadas and floodplains) are not appropriate analogs to interpret canal environments.

An important result of the Gila River canals modern analog study is that unique signatures from both pollen and micro-invertebrate data characterized individual contexts (Table 13). The biological signatures in canals were interpreted to reflect hydrologic environments, a conclusion supported by the soil particle size analyses from canal samples. The dynamic interaction between the biological assemblages and hydraulic character of individual canals could be better understood. A missing link in this study is data on the physical and chemical water environment in each canal. The sediment samples were collected during the winter when water was shut off to canals for maintenance. We have interpreted pollen and micro-invertebrate signatures to relate to different hydrologic environments, and the interpretations are consistent with the size and shape of the canals and sample sediment texture, but we acknowledge that direct water measurements are needed.

Implications for the Archaeological Record

Multidisciplinary studies such as these can provide very powerful tools to understand environments used or occupied by humans in the past. Paired pollen and micro-invertebrate samples from canals and other fluvial environments on GRIC lands, coupled with sediment particle size analysis, offer both independent and complementary perspectives on canal systems. Archaeologists interested in acquiring these data sets should focus on sediments with relatively low proportions of sand particles. The relationship between sediment particle size and organism recovery is similar for pollen and micro-invertebrates.

According to our study, archaeologists can expect canals of different ranks to have unique pollen signatures, reflecting pollen of varied geographic scales. Canal pollen samples poorly record local vegetation, which could be a helpful indicator for evaluating certain obscure features on the landscape as canal segments versus other possible pit features. Agricultural pollen types are preserved to a limited extent in canals, reinforcing the chances for identifying crops grown in fields in the vicinity of past canal systems. Micro-invertebrate assemblages of these modern canals share similarities with those recovered from prehistoric and historical canals, lending support to the usefulness of modern analogs for interpreting the past. Coupling ostracode with mollusc analysis lends additional support to interpretations, as

52

Table 13. Summary of Conclusions and Insights from This Study

Conclusions	Pollen Insights	Micro-invertebrate Insights
Canals are discriminated from other fluvial locations.	A regional, water-transported pollen signature characterizes canals, composed of pine, pinyon pine, juniper, and oak. Other key canal pollen types are cattail, willow, jojoba, mesquite, and prickly pear. The driest sites, McClellan Wash and Twin Buttes fan, are discriminated by low conifer pollen, no oak, no water indicators, and high Low-Spine Asteraceae, with hopbush, pecan, and plantain. Gila River and Little Gila River are intermediate between canals and the dry sites. Regional conifers, cattail, willow, jojoba, hopbush, spiderling, pecan, and plantain characterize the rivers.	No micro-invertebrates from the driest site, Twin Buttes fan (CS12). McClellan Wash also reflects dry to ephemeral conditions, based on fragmented mollusc shells (transported assemblages) and few ostracodes. Canals are characterized by reworked mollusc shells suggesting transported assemblages (allochthonous), but local ostracode populations (autochthonous) represent primarily freshwater stream species.
Unique biological assemblages characterize canals of different rank (size).	Pima Lateral (largest canal) has highest regional pollen (conifers and oak) and minimum pollen concentration. Northside (main canal) has second highest representation of regional pollen, with moderate pollen concentration. Mish Ki (distribution canal) has lowest regional pollen from canal contexts, highest extra-local and local types (mesquite, jojoba, cattail, and prickly pear), and low pollen concentration.	Pima Lateral canal has low diversity and abundance of micro-invertebrates. Northside has highest diversity and abundance of both molluscs and ostracodes. Mish Ki has lowest diversity and abundance of molluscs and ostracodes. Mish Ki micro-invertebrate assemblages record mixed conditions ranging from fresh, fast water to slow, saline conditions.
In canals, there is a relationship between the abundance and composition of biological assemblages and sediment particle size data, interpreted to reflect the hydrologic history of each canal. The integrated multidisciplinary results provide a more detailed reconstruction than individual datasets.	Pima Lateral (largest main canal): sandiest sediments indicate turbulent flow; micro-invertebrate data indicates high-energy, turbulent flow; low pollen concentration indicates turbulent flow; micro-invertebrate data indicate stable, moderately high-energy flows. Northside Canal (main canal): sediments predominantly silt and clay, indicate low-energy flows; moderate pollen concentration and regional pollen percentages consistent with lower-energy fluvial system; micro-invertebrate results interpreted to reflect low- to moderately low-energy conditions associated with permanent, long-term stable flow. Mish Ki Canal (distribution canal): sandy sediments indicate high-energy flow, turbulent flow; low pollen concentration supports interpretation of high-energy flow, but pollen assemblage mixed; micro-invertebrate data clearly indicate mixed hydrology (fast- to slow-energy conditions).	
Canal clean-out samples provide limited insights.	Mixed water and terrestrial types. Not recommended for canal studies, except possibly to assist in separating a clean-out deposit from canal sediments.	Micro-invertebrates in canal clean-out samples provide no useful insights; high shell fragmentation suggests destruction.
Other insights	Agricultural pollen types are recovered from canals, but it is unclear what the source area (local or extra-local) and vector (air or water) mechanisms are. Local pollen types are better represented in the terrestrial contexts; regional pollen types characterize canals and fluvial sites.	Freshwater mussel, *Anodonta californiensis*, common in prehistoric canal sediments but missing in modern Gila River canals. Possibly extirpated due to 20th century land-use impacts.

canals of different ranks have unique micro-invertebrate signatures, reflecting differing energy conditions. Samples from non-canal fluvial locations preserve assemblages that likewise suggest transport conditions and can differentiate canals from natural fluvial conditions.

Future Canal Studies

Analysis of prehistoric canal sediments for biological remains and sediment properties provides a means to examine and reconstruct components of prehistoric irrigation canal systems. Some additional questions of archaeological interest still need to be addressed. Future studies should include sampling actively flowing canals and acquisition of physical parameters of the water (water temperature, pH, conductivity, major and minor ions, streamflow velocity) to link assemblages to known water conditions at the time of deposition. By sampling canals in multiple seasons, the hydrologic parameters and organisms can be tied to periods of the calendar year, providing distinct seasonality signatures. The nature and timing of maintenance activities, specifically focusing on the use of fire to reduce canalside vegetation, might be documented through increased charcoal in pollen samples acquired downstream from headgates where fires are still used on occasion to clear vegetation masses. Acquisition of pollen samples and vegetation lists from slightly distant terrestrial loci will continue to reveal the potential contributions of airborne and locally available pollen to the landscape, for contrast to pollen within the canals. These studies should help refine the relationships between modern irrigation canals and the biological organisms and sediments within them, which can then serve as a strong proxy record for archaeological interpretation of prehistoric and historical canal conditions and use.

The synthesis of previous Hohokam canal studies offered here provides a means to focus future canal analysis on the Gila River Indian Community and elsewhere. Depending on the research questions of importance, micro-invertebrates, pollen, macro plant remains, and sediment studies will together or separately be most appropriate for analysis. Topics covered to date have included the evolution of irrigation technology, determining signatures that distinguish water-related features from other cultural loci, and a variety of aspects reflecting canal operation and construction. Similar analysis of reasonable numbers of samples from clearly defined pre-Classic and Classic period canals will be a crucial step in determining changing trends in irrigation systems through time, currently a significant gap in the literature.

REFERENCES CITED

Ackerly, N. W., J. B. Howard, and T. R. McGuire
1987   *La Ciudad Canals: A Study of Hohokam Irrigation Systems at the Community Level*. Anthropological Field Studies No. 17. Arizona State University, Tempe.

Ackerly, N. W., J. E. Kisselburg, and R. J. Martynec
1989   Canal Junctions and Water Control Features. In *Prehistoric Agricultural Activities on the Lehi-Mesa Terrace: Perspectives on Hohokam Irrigation Cycles*, edited by N. W. Ackerly and T. K. Henderson, pp. 146–183. Northland Research, Flagstaff.

Ahlstrom, R.V.N., and L. S. Cummings
1998   Blowing in the Wind? The Dispersal of Cotton Pollen in the Safford Valley, Arizona. Abstracts, Society of Ethnobiology, 21st Annual Conference, April 15–18, 1998. University of Nevada, Reno.

Antevs, E.
1941   *Age of the Cochise Cultural Stages*. Medallion Papers No. 29, pp. 31–81. Gila Pueblo, Globe, Arizona.

Barber, R. J.
1984   Land Snails, Freshwater Mollusks, and Environmental Reconstruction along the Salt-Gila Aqueduct. In *Hohokam Archaeology along the Salt-Gila Aqueduct*, Vol. 7: *Environment and Subsistence*, edited by L. S. Teague and P. L. Crown, pp. 95–108. Archaeological Series No. 150. Arizona State Museum, Tucson.

Bayman, F., M. R. Palacios-Fest, and L. W. Huckell
1997   Botanical Signatures of Water Storage Duration in a Hohokam Reservoir. *American Antiquity* 62(1):103–111.

Bequaert, J. C., and W. B. Miller
1973   *The Mollusks of the Arid Southwest*. University of Arizona Press, Tucson.

Bohrer, V. L.
1970   Ethnobotanical Aspects of Snaketown, a Hohokam Village in Southern Arizona. *American Antiquity* 35(4):413–430.

1992   New Life from Ashes II: A Tale of Burnt Bush. *Desert Plants* 19(3):122–125.

Bonny, A. B.
1978   The Effect of Pollen Recruitment Processes on Pollen Distribution over the Sediment Surface of a Small Lake in Cumbria. *Journal of Ecology* 66:385–416.

Bradbury, J. P., R. M. Forester, W. A. Bryant, and A. P. Covich
1987   Paleolimnology of Laguna de Cocos, Albion Island, Rio Hondo, Belize. In *Ancient Maya Wetland Agriculture: Excavations on Albion Island, Northern Belize,* edited by M. DeLand Pohl, pp. 119–154. Westview Press, Boulder, Colorado.

Bradley, R. S.
1999   *Paleoclimatology: Reconstructing Climates of the Quaternary.* 2nd ed. Academic Press, San Diego.

Brush, G., and L. M. Brush
1972   Transport of Pollen in a Sediment-Laden Channel: A Laboratory Study. *American Journal of Science* 272:359–381.

Cantley, G. J.
1991   *Archaeology of a Rockpile Field in the Santan Mountains, Arizona.* Unpublished master's thesis, Department of Anthropology, Arizona State University, Tempe.

Crowder, A., and D. G. Cuddy
1973   Pollen in a Small River Basin: Wilton Creek. In *Quaternary Plant Ecology,* edited by B.J.B. Birks and R. G. West, pp. 61–77. Blackwell, Oxford.

Crown, P.
1984   Prehistoric Agricultural Technology in the Salt-Gila Basin. In *Hohokam Archaeology along the Salt-Gila Aqueduct,* Vol. 7: *Environment and Subsistence,* edited by L. S. Teague and P. L. Crown, pp. 207–260. Archaeological Series No. 150. Arizona State Museum, Tucson.

1987   Classic Period Hohokam Settlement and Land Use in the Casa Grande Ruins Area, Arizona. *Journal of Field Archaeology* 14:147–162.

Curtis, J. H., M. Brenner, D. A. Hodell, R. A. Balser
1995   A Multi-proxy Study of Holocene Environmental Change in the Maya Lowlands of Peten, Guatemala. *Journal of Paleolimnology* 19:139–159.

Davis, M. B., and L. B. Brubaker
1973   Differential Sedimentation of Pollen Grains in Lakes. *Limnology and Oceanography* 18(4):635–646.

Delorme, L. D.
1969   Ostracodes as Quaternary Paleoecological Indicators. *Canadian Journal of Earth Sciences* 6:1471–1476.

1970   Freshwater Ostracodes of Canada, Part 3: Family Candonidae. *Canadian Journal of Zoology* 48:1099–1127.

1989   Methods in Quaternary Ecology No. 7: Freshwater Ostracodes. *Geoscience Canada* 16(2):85–90.

Dobyns, H. F.
1981   *From Fire to Flood: Historic Human Destruction of Sonoran Desert Riverine Oases.* Ballena Press Anthropological Papers 20. Socorro, New Mexico.

Doolittle, W. E.
1990   *Canal Irrigation in Prehistoric Mexico: The Sequence of Technological Change.* University of Texas Press, Austin.

Doyel, D. E.
1979   The Prehistoric Hohokam of the Arizona Desert. *American Scientist* 76(5):544–554.

Eugster, H. P., and L. A. Hardie
1978   Saline Lakes. In *Lakes: Chemistry, Geology, Physics*, edited by A. Lerman, pp. 237–293. Springer-Verlag, New York.

Eyles, N., and H. P. Schwarcz
1991 Stable Isotope Records of the Last Glacial Cycle from Lacustrine Ostracodes. *Geology* 19:257–260.

Faegri, K., and J. Iversen
1989   *Textbook of Pollen Analysis.* 4th ed. John Wiley & Sons, New York.

Faegri, K., and L. van der Pijl
1979   *The Principles of Pollination Ecology.* 3rd ed. Pergamon Press, Oxford.

Fall, P.
1987   Pollen Taphonomy in a Canyon Stream. *Quaternary Research* 28:393–406.

Fish, S. K.
1981   Palynological Results from Las Colinas. In *Report of the Testing of Interstate 10 Corridor Prehistoric and Historic Archaeological Remains between Interstate 17 and 30th drive (Group II, Las Colinas)*, edited by K. J. Schreiber, C. H. McCarthy, and B. Byrd, pp. 245–251. Archaeological Series No. 156. Arizona State Museum, Tucson.

1983   Pollen from Agricultural Features. In *Hohokam Archaeology along the Salt-Gila Aqueduct*, Vol. 3: *Specialized Activity Sites, Part IV, Agricultural Features*, edited by L. S. Teague and P. L. Crown, pp. 575–603. Archaeological Series No. 150: Arizona State Museum, Tucson.

1986   Appendix B: Pollen Results from the Swilling's Ditch.. In *The Archaeology of Swilling's Ditch: Phoenix's First Historic Canal*, edited by J. S. Cable and D. E. Doyel, pp. 49–54. Anthropological Papers No. 2 . Pueblo Grande Museum, Phoenix.

1987   Pollen Results from the Las Acequias–Los Muertos Irrigation System and Related Features. In *Archaeological Investigations of Portions of the Las Acequias–Los Muertos Irrigation System*, edited by W. B. Masse, pp. 159–167. Archaeological Series No. 176. Arizona State Museum, Tucson.

1997   Modeling Human Impacts to the Borderlands Environment from a Fire Ecology Perspective. In *Effects of Fire on Madrean Province Ecosystems, a Symposium Proceedings*, edited by H. Hambre, pp. 125–134. USDA General Technical Report RM-GTR-289.Rocky Mountain Region, Fort Collins, CO.

1998   Archaeological Palynology of Gardens and Fields. In *The Archaeology of Garden and Field*, edited by N. F. Miller and G. L. Bleason, pp. 44–69. University of Pennsylvania Press, Philadelphia.

2000   Hohokam Impacts on Sonoran Desert Environment. In *Imperfect Balance: Landscape Transformations in the Precolumbian Americas*, edited by D. L. Lentz, pp. 251–280. Columbia University Press, New York.

Forester, R. M.
1988   Nonmarine Calcareous Microfossils Sample Preparation and Data Acquisition Procedures. In *U.S. Geological Survey Technical Procedure, HP-78*, R1, pp. 1–9.

1991   Ostracode Assemblages from Springs in the Western United States: Implications for Paleohydrology. *Memoirs of the Entomological Society of Canada* 155, pp. 181–200.

Foster, M. S.
2000   *A Cultural Resources Testing Program at 32 Proposed Home Sites on the Gila River Indian Community, Maricopa and Pinal Counties, Arizona.* CRMP Technical Report No. 2000-02. Cultural Resource Management Program, Gila River Indian Community, Sacaton.

Gish, J. W.
1978   Pollen Results from the Los Hornos Site, Central Arizona. Ms. on file, Office of Cultural Resource Management, Department of Anthropology, Arizona State University, Tempe.

1979a The Los Aumentos Pollen Study. Ms. on file, Museum of Northern Arizona, Flagstaff.

1979b Appendix C: Cave Buttes Dam Mitigation, Arizona, a Palynological Perspective. In *Archaeological Investigations in the Cave Creek Area, Maricopa County, South-Central Arizona*, edited by T. K. Henderson and J. B. Rodgers, pp. 158–179. Anthropological Research Paper No. 17. Arizona State University, Tempe.

1984   Pollen Analysis of the Murphy's Addition. In *City of Phoenix, Archaeology of the Original Townsite: The Murphy's Addition: Block 28-North*, edited by J. S. Cable, S. L.

Henry, and D. E. Doyel, pp. 195–213. Publications in Archaeology No. 3. Soil Systems, Phoenix.

1985   Pollen from the New River Project, and a Discussion of Pollen Sampling Strategies for Agricultural Systems. In *Hohokam Settlement and Economic Systems in the Central New River Drainage, Arizona*, edited by D. E. Doyel and M. D. Elson, pp. 343–403. Soil Systems Publications in Archaeology No. 4. Phoenix.

1988   Casa Buena Pollen Analysis. In *Excavations at Casa Buena: Changing Hohokam Land Use along the Squaw Peak Parkway, Vol. 2*, edited by J. B. Howard, pp. 587–603. Soil Systems Publications in Archaeology No. 11. Phoenix.

1989   A Pollen Evaluation of the Las Acequias Canal System. In *Prehistoric Agricultural Activities on the Lehi-Mesa Terrace: Perspectives on Hohokam Irrigation Cycles*, edited by N. W. Ackerly and T. K. Henderson, pp. 279–332. Northland Research, Flagstaff.

1991   Current Perceptions, Recent Discoveries, and Future Directions in Hohokam Palynology. *Kiva* 56(3):237–254.

Goman, M., and R. Byrne
1998   A 5,000-Year Record of Agriculture and Tropical Forest Clearance in the Tuxtlas, Veracruz, Mexico. *Holocene* 8(1): 83–89.

Graybill, D. A., D. A. Gregory, G. S. Funkhouser, and F. L. Nials
1999   Long-Term Streamflow Reconstructions, River Channel Morphology, and Aboriginal Irrigation Systems along the Salt and Gila Rivers. In *Environmental Change and Human Adaptation in the Ancient Southwest*, edited by J. S. Dean and D. E. Doyel. University of Utah Press, in preparation.

Gregory, D. A., and G. Huckleberry
1994   *An Archaeological Survey of the Blackwater Area, Vol. 1: The History of Human Settlement in the Blackwater Area*. Cultural Resources Report No. 86. Archaeological Consulting Services, Tempe.

Grim, Eric
1987   CONISS: A Fortran 77 Program for Stratigraphically Constrained Cluster Analysis by the Method of Incremental Sum of Squares. *Computers & Geosciences* 13(1):13–35.

Haury, E. W.
1937   The Snaketown Canal. In *Excavations at Snaketown: Material Culture*, edited by H. S. Gladwin, E. W. Haury, E. S. Sayles, and N. Gladwin, pp. 50–58. Medallion Papers No. 25. Gila Pueblo, Globe, Arizona.

1976   *The Hohokam: Desert Farmers and Craftsmen*. University of Arizona Press, Tucson.

Hevly, R. H., P. J. Mehringer, Jr., and H. G. Yocum
1965 Modern Pollen Rain in the Sonoran Desert. *Journal of the Arizona Academy of Science* 3:123–135.

Howard, J. B.
1990 *Paleohydraulics: Techniques for Modeling the Operation and Growth of Prehistoric Canal Systems.* Unpublished master's thesis, Department of Anthropology, Arizona State University, Tempe.

Howard, J. B., and G. A. Huckleberry
1991 *The Operations and Evolution of an Irrigation System: The East Papago Canal Study.* Soil Systems Publications in Archaeology No. 18. Phoenix.

Huckleberry, G. A.
1993 *Late-Holocene Stream Dynamics on the Middle Gila River, Pinal County, Arizona.* Unpublished Ph.D. dissertation, Department of Geosciences, University of Arizona, Tucson

1999 Assessing Hohokam Canal Stability through Stratigraphy. *Journal of Field Archaeology* 26:1-1.

Kearney, T. H., and R. H. Peebles
1960 *Arizona Flora.* 2nd ed., with supplement. University of California Press, Berkeley.

Lytle-Webb, J.
1981 Pollen Analysis of Irrigation Canals. *Kiva* 47(1–2):83–90.

Mabry, J. B.
1996 *Canals and Communities: small scale irrigation systems.* University of Arizona Press, Tucson.

Masse, W. B.
1991 The Quest for Subsistence Sufficiency and Civilization in the Sonoran Desert. In *Chaco and Hohokam: Prehistoric Regional Systems in the American Southwest*, edited by P. L. Crown and W. J. Judge, pp. 195–223. School of American Research Press, Santa Fe.

McLaughlin, D.
1976 Report on Analysis of Pollen Samples from Hohokam Irrigation Canal Sites, AZ U:9:2, AZ U:9:28, and AZ U:9:26. In *The Hohokam Expressway Project: A Study of Prehistoric Irrigation in the Salt River Valley, Arizona*, W. B. Masse, with contributions by R. E. Gasser, M. T. Keller and D. McLaughlin. pp. 64–76. Arizona State Museum Contributions, Highway Salvage Archaeology No. 43. Tucson.

Midvale, F.
1946 The Prehistoric Canals and Ruins of the Casa Grande–Florence Area of the Gila River in Southern Arizona. Map on file, Frank Midvale Collection, Department of Archives and Manuscripts, Hayden Library, Arizona State University, Tempe.

1963 The Prehistoric Irrigation of the Casa Grande Ruins Area of the Gila River in Southern Arizona. Map on file (No. 225), Frank Midvale Collection, Department of Archives and Manuscripts, Hayden Library, Arizona State University, Tempe.

Miksicek, C. H.
1983 Appendix B. Plant Remains from Agricultural Features. In *Hohokam Archaeology along the Salt-Gila Aqueduct Central Arizona Project,* Vol. 3: *Specialized Activity Sites,* edited by L. S. Teague and P. L. Crown, pp. 604–620. Archaeological Series No. 150. Arizona State Museum, Tucson.

1985 Unpublished data from Las Colinas Project (1984) on file with the Cultural Resources Management Division, Arizona State Museum, Tucson.

1987 Wood Charcoal and Seeds. In *Archaeological Investigations of Portions of Las Acequias–Los Muertos Irrigation System,* edited by W. B. Masse, pp. 169–175. Archaeological Series No. 176. Arizona State Museum, Tucson.

1989 Snails, Seeds, and Charcoal: Macrofossils from the Las Acequias Canal System. In *Prehistoric Agricultural Activities on the Lehi-Mesa Terrace: Perspectives on Hohokam Irrigation Cycles,* edited by N. W. Ackerly and T. K. Henderson, pp. 235–262. Northland Research, Flagstaff.

1995 Canal Mollusks and Plant Remains. In *Archaeology at the Head of the Scottsdale Canal System,* Vol. 3: *Canal and Synthetic Studies,* edited by M. R. Hackbarth and T. K. Henderson, pp. 121–131. Anthropological Papers No. 95-1. Northland Research, Phoenix.

Mitalsky [Midvale], F.
1935 A General Map of the Central Pima Country on the Gila. Prepared for Arizona Geography Course. Ms. on file, Cultural Resource Management Program, Gila River Indian Community, Sacaton.

Moore, P. D., J. A. Webb, and M. E. Collinson
1991 *Pollen Analysis.* 2nd ed. Blackwell Scientific Publications, Cambridge.

Neily, R. B.
1997 *A Cultural Resource Survey of the Proposed Santan to Roosevelt Water Conservation District (RWCD) Canal, Santan Management Area, Pima-Maricopa Irrigation Project (P-MIP), Gila River Indian Community, Arizona.* P-MIP Technical

Report No. 97-03. Cultural Resource Management Program, Gila River Indian Community, Sacaton.

Neily, R. B., M. Brodbeck, and K. S. Wigglesworth
1999   *An Archaeological Survey of the Santan Canal Reaches and Adjoining Areas in the Santan Management Area, Pima-Maricopa Irrigation Project (P-MIP), Gila River Indian Community, Arizona.* P-MIP Report No. 2. Cultural Resource Management Program, Gila River Indian Community, Sacaton.

Neily, R. B., B. G. Randolph, S. R. James, and M. Brodbeck
2000   *An Archaeological Assessment of the Southwestern Portion of the Santan Management Area, Pima-Maricopa Irrigation Project (P-MIP), Gila River Indian Community, Arizona.* P-MIP Report No. 10. Cultural Resource Management Program, Gila River Indian Community, Sacaton.

Nials, F. L., and S. Fish
1988   Canals and Related Features. In *The 1982–1984 Excavations at Las Colinas: The Site and Its Features*, D. A. Gregory, W. L. Deaver, S. K. Fish, R. Gardiner, R. W. Layhe, F. L. Nials, and L. S. Teague, pp. 275–305. Archaeological Series No. 162(2). Arizona State Museum, Tucson.

Palacios-Fest, M. R.
1989   Late Holocene Ostracodes as Hydrochemical Indicators in the Phoenix Basin. In *Prehistoric Agricultural Activities on the Lehi-Mesa Terrace: Perspectives on Hohokam Irrigation Cycles*, edited by N. W. Ackerly and T. K. Henderson, pp. 263–278. Northland Research, Flagstaff.

1994   Nonmarine Ostracode Shell Chemistry from Ancient Hohokam Irrigation Canals in Central Arizona: A Paleohydrochemical Tool for the Interpretation of Prehistoric Human Occupation in the North American Southwest. *Geoarchaeology: An International Journal* 9:1–29.

1995   Continental Ostracode Record in the Scottsdale System. In *Archaeological Excavations at Pueblo Blanco: The MCDOT Alma School Road Project*, edited by D. E. Doyel, pp. 363–392. Archaeological Consulting Services, Phoenix.

1996a   Hohokam Canal Ostracode Paleoenvironments from the McDowell-to-Shea Sites. In *Archaeology at the Head of the Scottsdale Canal System*, Vol. 3, *Canal and Synthetic Studies*, edited by M. R. Hackbarth, T. K. Henderson and D. B. Craig. Northland Research, Inc., Flagstaff.

1996b   Site AA:12:753 (Ina Road and I-10 Canals): Early Irrigation Systems in Southeastern Arizona and the Ostracode Perspective. Ms on file, Desert Archaeology, Tucson.

1997a Paleoenvironmental Reconstruction of Human Activity in Central Arizona Using Shell Chemistry of Hohokam Canal Ostracodes. *Geoarchaeology: An International Journal* 12:211–226.

1997b Pecos Road Testing Project 97.12, GR-556: The Microinvertebrate Record. Ms. on file, Cultural Resource Management Program, Gila River Indian Community, Sacaton, Arizona.

1997c Continental Ostracode Paleoecology from the Hohokam Pueblo Blanco Area, Central Arizona. *Journal of Archaeological Science* 24: 965–983.

1997d Reconstruction of Hohokam Canal Paleoecology from La Cuenca del Sedimento, Tempe, Arizona. Report submitted to Northland Research, Flagstaff.

1997e Evidence of Hohokam Agriculture Based on the Occurrence of Continental Ostracodes. Report submitted to Western Cultural Resources Management, Tempe, AZ

1997f Ostracode Paleoecology from a Phoenix Site, Arizona. Arizona MP-F. State Museum, Tucson. Report submitted to Dr. Paul Fish, University of Arizona.

1999a Site AZ AA:12:753 (Ina Road & I-10): Early Irrigation Systems in Southeastern Arizona and the Ostracode Perspective. Report prepared for Dr. Jonathan Mabry, Center for Desert Archaeology, Tucson.

1999b Ostracode Evidence in Hohokam Reservoirs. Report prepared for Dr. James Bayman, Department of Anthropology, University of Hawaii–Manoa, Honolulu.

Palacios-Fest, M. R., A. S. Cohen, and P. Anadón
1994 Use of Ostracodes as Paleoenvironmental Tools in the Interpretation of Ancient Lacustrine Records. *Revista Española de Paleontología* 9(2):145–164.

Palacios-Fest, M. R., J. B. Mabry, F. Nials, J. P. Holmlund, E. Miksa, and O. K. Davis
2001 Early Irrigation Systems in Southeastern Arizona: The Ostracode Perspective. *Journal of South American Earth Sciences* 14:541–555.

Peck, R. M.
1973 Pollen Budget Studies in a Small Yorkshire Catchment. In *Quaternary Plant Ecology*, edited by B.J.B. Birks and R. G. West, pp. 43–61. Blackwell, Oxford.

Pennington, W.
1979 The Origin of Pollen in Lake Sediments: An Enclosed Lake Compared with One Receiving Inflow Streams. *New Phytologist* 83:189–213.

Pfaff, C.

1994 *The San Carlos Irrigation Project: An Historic Overview and Evaluation of Significance, Pinal County, Arizona.* Technical Services Center, Bureau of Reclamation, Denver.

1996 *San Carlos Irrigation Project, North and South of Gila River, Vicinity of Coolidge, Pinal County, Arizona: Photographs, Written Historical, and Descriptive Data.* Historic American Engineering Record No. AZ-50. Technical Services Center, Bureau of Reclamation, Denver.

Phillips, B. G. and D. B. Craig

2001 Canals. In The Grewe Archaeological Research Project, Volume 1: Project Background and Feature Descriptions, edited by Douglas B. Craig, pp. 147-162. Anthropological Papers No. 99-1. Northland Research, Inc., Flagstaff and Tempe.

Pokorný, V.

1978 Ostracodes. In *Introduction to Marine Micropaleontology*, edited by B. U. Haq and A. Boersma, pp. 109–149. Elsevier North Holland, New York.

Puleston, D. E.

1977 The Art and Archaeology of Hydraulic Agriculture in the Maya Lowlands. In *Social Process in Maya Prehistory*, edited by Norman Hammond, pp. 445–476. Academic Press, London.

Rea, A. M.

1983 *Once a River: Bird Life and Habitat Changes on the Middle Gila.* University of Arizona Press, Tucson.

1997 *At the Desert's Green Edge: An Ethnobotany of the Gila River Pima.* University of Arizona Press, Tucson.

San Carlos Irrigation Project (SCIP)

1983 Annual Irrigation Report, Calendar Year 1982. San Carlos Irrigation Project, Coolidge, Arizona.

1984 Annual Irrigation Report, Calendar Year 1983. San Carlos Irrigation Project, Coolidge, Arizona.

1985 Annual Irrigation Report, Calendar Year 1984. San Carlos Irrigation Project, Coolidge, Arizona.

1986 Annual Irrigation Report, Calendar Year 1985. San Carlos Irrigation Project, Coolidge, Arizona.

1987 Annual Irrigation Report, Calendar Year 1986. San Carlos Irrigation Project, Coolidge, Arizona.

1988   Annual Irrigation Report, Calendar Year 1987.   San Carlos Irrigation Project, Coolidge, Arizona.

1989   Annual Irrigation Report, Calendar Year 1988.   San Carlos Irrigation Project, Coolidge, Arizona.

1990   Annual Irrigation Report, Calendar Year 1989.   San Carlos Irrigation Project, Coolidge, Arizona.

1991   Annual Irrigation Report, Calendar Year 1990.   San Carlos Irrigation Project, Coolidge, Arizona.

1992   Annual Irrigation Report, Calendar Year 1991.   San Carlos Irrigation Project, Coolidge, Arizona.

1993   Annual Irrigation Report, Calendar Year 1992.   San Carlos Irrigation Project, Coolidge, Arizona.

1999   Annual Irrigation Report, Calendar Year 1998.   San Carlos Irrigation Project, Coolidge, Arizona.

2000 Annual Irrigation Report, Calendar Year 1999.   San Carlos Irrigation Project, Coolidge, Arizona.

Schoenwetter, J.
  1980   The Los Hornos Pollen Study. Ms. on file, Department of Anthropology, Arizona State University, Tempe.

Schoenwetter, J., and L. A. Doerschlag
  1971   Surficial Pollen Records from Central Arizona, I: Sonoran Desert Scrub. *Journal of the Arizona Academy of Science* 6(3):216–221.

Sheridan, T. E.
  1988   *Where the Dove Calls: The Political Ecology of a Peasant Corporate Community in Northwestern Mexico*. University of Arizona Press, Tucson.

Shreve, F., and I. L. Wiggins
  1964   *Vegetation and Flora of the Sonoran Desert*. Volumes 1 and 2. Stanford University Press, Stanford, CA.

Smith, S.
  1995   Pollen Analysis of the MTS Canals. In *Archaeology at the Head of the Scottsdale Canal System*, Vol. 3: *Canal and Synthetic Studies,* edited by M. Hackbarth, K. Henderson, and D. B. Craig, pp. 105–120. Anthropological Papers No. 95-1. Northland Research, Tempe.

1997a Pollen Analysis of Six Samples, Canal Rio, Durango Street Monitoring Project. Ms. on file, Northland Research, Tempe.

1997b Pollen Analysis of Nine Canal Samples, Pecos Road Testing Project, GR-556. Ms. on file, Cultural Resource Management Program, Gila River Indian Community, Sacaton.

1997c Pollen Analysis of Eleven Prehistoric Canal Samples, Mesa City Sound Barrier Project. Report submitted to Mark Hackbarth, Northland Research, Tempe.

Solomon, A. M., T. J. Blasing, and J. A. Solomon
1982 Interpretation of Floodplain Pollen in Alluvial Sediments from an Arid Region. *Quaternary Research* 18:52–71.

Starling, R. N., and A. Crowder
1981 Pollen in the Salmon River System, Ontario, Canada. *Review of Palaeobotany and Palynology* 31:311–334.

Turner, R. M., J. E. Bowers, T. L. Burgess
1995 *Sonoran Desert Plants: An Ecological Atlas*. University of Arizona Press, Tucson.

Vokes, A. W., and C. H. Miksicek
1987 Snails, Clams, and Canals: An Analysis of Nonmarine Molluscan Remains. In *Archaeological Investigations of Portions of the Las Acequias–Los Muertos Irrigation System: Testing and Partial Data Recovery within the Tempe Section of the Outer Loop Freeway System, Maricopa County, Arizona,* edited by W. B. Masse, pp. 177–187. Archaeological Series No. 176. Arizona State Museum, Tucson.

Waters, M. R.
1988 Holocene Alluvial Geology and Geoarchaeology of the San Xavier Reach of the Santa Cruz River, Arizona. *Geological Society of America Bulletin* 100:479–491.

1996 *Surficial Geologic Map of the Gila River Indian Community*. P-MIP Technical Report No. 96-1. Cultural Resource Management Program, Gila River Indian Community, Sacaton.

Waters, M. R., and J. C. Ravesloot
2000 Late Quaternary Geology of the Middle Gila River, Gila River Indian Reservation, Arizona. *Quaternary Research* 54:49–57.

2001 Landscape Changes and the Cultural Evolution of the Hohokam along the Middle Gila River and Other River Valleys in South-Central Arizona. *American Antiquity* 66(2):285–299.

Webb, W. F.

1942 *United States Mollusca: A Descriptive Manual of Many Marine, Land, and Fresh Water Shells of North America, North of Mexico.* Lee Publications, Wellesley Hills, Massachusetts.

Wilcox, D. R.

1979 The Hohokam Regional System. In *An Archaeological Test of Sites in the Gila Butte–Santan Region, South-Central Arizona,* edited by G. Rice, D. Wilcox, K. Rafferty, and J. Schoenwetter, pp. 77–177. University Anthropological Research Papers No. 18. Arizona State University, Tempe.

Wilson, J. P.

1999 Peoples of the Middle Gila: A Documentary History of the Pimas and Maricopas, 1500s–1945. Ms. on file, Cultural Resource Management Program, Gila River Indian Community, Sacaton, Arizona.

Wiseman, F. M.

1983 Analysis of Pollen from the Fields at Pulltrouser Swamp. In *Pulltrouser Swamp: Ancient Maya Habitat, Agriculture, and Settlement in Northern Belize,* edited by B. L. Turner II and P. D. Harrison, pp. 105–119. University of Texas, Austin.

1990 San Antonio: A Late Holocene Record of Agricultural Activity in the Maya Lowlands. In *Ancient Maya Wetland Agriculture: Excavations on Albion Island, Northern Belize,* edited by M. D. Pohl, pp. 313–322. Westview Press, Boulder, Colorado.

Woodbury, R. B.

1961 A Reappraisal of Hohokam Irrigation. *American Anthropologist* 63:550–560.

Woodson, M. K.

2001a *A Preliminary Report on the Results of a Phase I Data Recovery Program Conducted in the Sweetwater Site (GR-931) and Adjacent Areas along State Route 587, Gila River Indian Community, Pinal County, Arizona.* CRMP Technical Report No. 2001-12. Cultural Resource Management Program, Gila River Indian Community, Sacaton.

2001b *A Preliminary Report on the Results of a Phase II Data Recovery Program Conducted in the Sweetwater Site (GR-931) along State Route 587, Gila River Indian Community, Pinal County, Arizona.* CRMP Technical Report No. 2001-21. Cultural Resource Management Program, Gila River Indian Community, Sacaton.

2002 *A Research Design for the Study of Prehistoric and Historical Irrigation Systems in the Middle Gila Valley, Arizona.* P-MIP Technical Report 2002-01. Cultural Resource Management Program, Gila River Indian Community, Sacaton.

68

Woodson, M. K., and E. Davis

2001   *A Cultural Resources Assessment of the Western Half of the Blackwater Management Area, P-MIP, Gila River Indian Community, Pinal County, Arizona.* P-MIP Report No. 14. Cultural Resource Management Program, Gila River Indian Community, Sacaton.

Woodson, M. K., and R. B. Neily

1998   *Cultural Resource Testing along the Pecos Road Segment of the Pecos-Price Canal Alignment, Santan Extension (Memorial) Management Area, P-MIP, Gila River Indian Community, Maricopa County, Arizona.* P-MIP Technical Report 97-08. Cultural Resource Management Program, Gila River Indian Community, Sacaton.

Woodson, M. K., and B. G. Randolph

2000   *National Register of Historic Places Eligibility Assessment of 67 Sites in the Blackwater Management Area,P-MIP, Gila River Indian Community, Pinal County, Arizona.* P-MIP Technical Report No. 00-03. Cultural Resource Management Program, Gila River Indian Community, Sacaton.

APPENDIX

Pollen Results, Mollusc Results, Ostracodes Results

Appen

	9	10		60	61	70	71
Specimen Number	9	10		28	28	33	33
Plant Collecting Station (CS)	4	4					
Context	Northside Canal fill	Northside Canal fill	N.d. C n in)	E area McClellan Wash (grassy area)	W area McClellan Wash (grassy area)	Little Gila River E of road	Little Gila River W of road
Particle Size (% sand)	6.4	43.2		54.4	23.4	46.4	46.4
Particle Size (% silt)	68.0	23.8		32.0	47.0	40.0	40.0
Particle Size (% clay)	25.6	33.0		13.6	29.6	13.6	13.6
Sample Volume (cc)	20	20		20	20	20	20
Pollen Sum	253	254		280	280	211	247
Pollen Conc. (gr/cc[a])	28846.6	45509.5		16722.7	43897.0	7561.0	28162.5
Tracers	11	7		21	8	35	11
Taxa Richness[b]	19	23		21	14	18	21
Pinus	2	3		2	2	3	1
Pinus (pinyon type)	8	10		3	3	1	1
Juniperus	6	19		9	3	11	1
Quercus	1	9		0	0	0	0
Juglans	0	0		0	0	0	0
Rosaceae	0	2		0	0	1	0
Artemisia	0	1		0	0	0	0
Celtis	0	3		0	0	0	2
Dodonaea	0	X[c]		1	1	1	0
Simmondsia	2	1		1	0	0	2
Ephedra	2	2		0	0	0	2
Rhamnaceae	1	0		0	0	0	0
Typha	0	1		0	0	1	0
Salix	0	6		0	0	19	0
Cyperaceae	0	0		0	0	2	0
Prosopis	0	3		1	0	0	0
Cercidium	0	0		2	1	0	0
Acacia	0	0		0	0	0	0
Larrea	4	0		0	0	0	0
Fouquieria	0	0		0	0	0	0
Sarcobatus	0	0		6	37	0	0
Cheno-am	124	64		132	153	67	124
Tidestroemia	0	1		0	0	0	0
Asteraceae	38	47		10	10	26	21

25	26	27	28	42	43	60	61	70	71
11	11	12	12	19	19	28	28	33	33
rg Rd. anal n-out	Olberg Rd. Canal clean-out	Holocene fan drainage	Holocene fan drainage (island)	E side Olberg Rd. (modern floodplain)	W side Olberg Rd. (modern floodplain)	E area McClellan Wash (grassy area)	W area McClellan Wash (grassy area)	Little Gila River E of road	Little Gila River W of road
0	0	0	0	0	0	0	0	0	0
0	1	0	0	0	0	0	0	X	1
38	13	151	97	27	98	35	30	23	19
21	10	27	36	35	38	44	32	23	50
1	1	0	0	1	2	0	0	1	1
0	0	0	0	0	0	0	0	0	0
0	0	0	0	1	0	X	0	0	0
0	0	0	2	3	0	0	0	0	1
1	3	1	0	3	X	1	0	1	1
0	0	2	2	1	1	3	2	3	0
0	0	X	0	0	X	0	0	0	X
4	1	2	3	11	6	2	2	1	3
0	0	1	0	0	1	7	0	0	5
0	0	0	0	0	0	0	X	0	0
0	0	0	0	0	0	0	0	0	0
0	0	1	0	0	0	0	0	0	0
0	0	0	0	0	X	0	0	0	0
0	1	0	0	0	0	0	0	0	1
0	0	0	0	0	0	0	0	0	0
0	0	0	0	1	0	0	0	0	0
0	0	X	0	1	0	0	0	0	0
0	0	X	X	0	X	0	0	0	X
0	0	0	0	0	X	0	0	0	X
0	0	0	0	0	0	X	0	0	0
0	0	X	X	0	0	0	0	0	0
0	0	X	1	0	0	0	0	0	0
0	0	0	0	1	6	1	0	0	X
0	X	1	X	0	1	X	0	0	0
0	0	0	X	0	0	0	0	0	0
X	0	X	1	0	X	1	1	X	0
28	3	2	12	22	10	8	2	18	4
4	1	3	6	3	5	11	1	8	3
0	0	0	0	0	0	0	0	0	4

Appendix T

Specimen Number	9	10		60	61	70	71
Plant Collecting Station (CS)	4	4		28	28	33	33
Context	Northside Canal fill	Northside Canal fill - C	Rd. m ain)	E area McClellan Wash (grassy area)	W area McClellan Wash (grassy area)	Little Gila River E of road	Little Gila River W of road
Total aggregates[e]	5	1		0	0	1	0
Cheno-am aggregates	5(30+)	0	)	0	0	0	0
Cheno-am aggregates from scans	0	0		0	0	0	0
Asteraceae aggregates	0	0		0	0	0	0
Ambrosia aggregates	0	0		0	0	0	0
Poaceae aggregates	0	1(6)	)	0	0	1(4)	0
Sphaeralcea aggregates	0	0		0	0	0	0
Juniperus aggregates	0	0		0	0	0	0
Pinus (pinyon type) aggregates	0	0		0	0	0	0
Ephedra aggregates	0	0		0	0	0	0
Trilete spores with perine	X	X		X	X	X	0

[a] Concentration is an estimate of the numb
  based on an initial tracer concentration (
[b] Taxa Richness is the number of pollen ty
[c] X denotes taxa identified during 100x sc
[d] Unknown A, possibly *Larrea* or *Tamari*
[e] Pollen aggregate notation shows the num

Other Groups:

Sample ID	Dry Wt.	Residue	Molluscs	Redox Index	Color	Plant Debris	Oogonia
	(g)	(g)					
CS4-9	76.35	1.37	18	0	Natural	X	X
CS4-10	85.93	9.41	22	1	White	X	
CS4-11	91.14	21.13	8	0	Natural	X	
CS4-12	128.36	4.85	10	1	White	X	
CS4-13	55.37	1.70	2	0	Natural	X	
CS5-14	127.10	116.00	27	0	Natural	X	
CS5-15	126.90	105.43	13	0	Natural	X	
CS5-16	126.11	18.58	2	0	Natural	X	
CS6-17	122.64	104.78	24	1	White	X	
CS6-18	121.78	11.59	51	1	White	X	X
CS6-19	126.37	57.57	9	1	White		
CS11-25	123.40	12.93	16	1	White	X	
CS11-26	123.58	19.24	4	0	Natural	X	
CS28-60	51.50	11.19	6	1	White	X	
CS28-61	54.28	2.88	4	1	White	X	
CS33-70	55.16	7.95	8	0	Natural	X	
CS33-71	52.59	13.99	5	0	Natural	X	

Abbreviation: cs = collecting station

Note: Also included are other biolog

ndance of Ostracodes Present in Samples.

C/V	A/J	Herpetocypris brevicaudata N	%	C/V	A/J	Candona caudata N	%	C/V	A/J	Cypria ophthalmica N	%	C/V	A/J	Unidentified N	%	C/V	A/J	Fragmentation	Encrustation	Coating	Abrasion	Redox Index	Color
		2	5	0	0													10	0	0	0	0	Clear
	1	3	6	0	0.33	6	13	0	0.17	1	2	0	0					15	0	0	0	0	Clear
	0	5	16	0	0.20									3	10	0	0.33	15	0	5	0	0	Clear
	0	21	15	0	0.05													15	0	0	0	1	Slightly orange
	0																	10	0	0	0	0	Clear
																		30	0	0	0	0	Clear
		1	50	0	1.00													5	0	0	0	0	Clear
		14	20	0.14	0.14													5	0	0	0	0	Clear
		2	67	0	1.00													60	0	0	0	0	Clear
		17	27	0	0													5	5	0	0	0	Clear
																		0	0	0	0	0	White
		2	9	0	0.50													5	0	0	0	0	Clear
		4	13	0	0.25													5	0	0	0	0	Clear
	0					1	25	0	0									25	5	5	10	1	Slightly orange

Taphonomy: